Keep Looking UP

Transforming Grief into Hope After Tragedy

CAREY CONLEY & LAUREL WILSON

LaCoCa Press

Dedicated to Ross and Cole Conley, two great men who left the world a better place. We look up to them with deep appreciation for the memories we created together and the joy they gave us, and still give us. Their purpose and impact on others are their legacy, and our role in it lives on.

Table of Contents

PREFACE

When my husband, Ross, taught our daughter to ride a bike, he told her to look up—and not at her feet—and keep her eyes toward where she was going. He would say, "Laurel, remember that you will always go in the direction your eyes take you. Your bike will follow your sight path."

After a wobbly start and a couple scraped knees, Laurel learned the hard way that she would lose her balance if she stared at her feet. She also discovered her eyes would take her right into a ditch or tree if she didn't keep them focused on where she wanted to go. She soon kept her head up and rode like the wind. Her father gave her the same sage advice when he taught her to ski, and she bombed down a mountain like a pro.

Ross's wisdom is as true in sports as it is in life, where we have to face even tougher challenges, such as the death of a loved one. The only way to make your way safely down a road or mountain, or through loss and grief, is to keep looking up. To get beyond the struggles immediately in front of us, we must raise our eyes to see a greater vision.

Today's results-oriented culture can make it difficult to keep our sights on the bigger picture in life. We are so focused on success that we groom our children for it from infancy onward. The best schools. The best teachers. The best jobs. We often walk through life with our heads down, focusing on all the small stuff, the little things we think are so monumentally important in order to achieve and display success. We get wrapped up in possessions, prestige, and superficial relationships. We come to believe that these things mark achievement, and that this type of success is so vital, we deny our true selves to create that result. Unfortunately, forsaking our identities can lead to anxiety and depression, even if material or social "success" is realized. This can drop us into a deep void. Once there, we might question the validity of our lives, which can eat us alive when we lose someone who truly matters.

An Uber driver once told me how he had lost his wife to a car accident four years earlier and was himself diagnosed with cancer two years later. He was about to start his second round of chemotherapy and was driving for Uber to pay his hospital bills. He had hoped to become a musician and had worked hard at his craft, believing he would have made it big in Nashville by that time. Instead, he was fighting for his life and giving rides to strangers to pay for his treatment. It was not the life he had envisioned.

We are told we will have great results if we do all the right things and work hard, and we are left unprepared when it all goes sideways. In our family, Laurel and I were blind-sided and devastated by two suicides: Ross, and my son, Cole. Through a long, painful journey, we learned the only way we could get through the day was to keep looking up to see the bigger picture and develop a clear perspective of what's important in life—and what's not.

Ross and Cole influenced our lives in major ways and made us who we are today, and their memory fuels our passion to carry out their legacies. We wrote this book with the purpose of helping others cope with the immediate aftermath of loss and grief. In each chapter, we share our story, insights, and message of hope. At the end of each chapter, we provide exercises in the form of reflections and questions to consider, either by yourself or in group discussions. We hope our book helps you to look up to a better place and create a vision that transforms your life so you can get excited about today and the future.

—*Carey Conley*

INTRODUCTION

The Conley family was like many others who worked hard to build wonderful and loving family lives. Their story began when Carey Wilson met Ross Conley in high school. They became lifelong sweethearts, dating throughout their college years at Oklahoma State University and attending dances hosted by each other's sorority and fraternity. Both of them were outgoing by nature, attracting a large tribe of friends throughout their school years and after. They married after graduation and settled in Colorado. Carey worked in the marketing field, and Ross worked in corporate sales for the same company for more than twenty years.

Blessed with successful careers, they bought a large house in a beautiful neighborhood.

As a young married couple, Ross and Carey cooked together, hosted game nights, and traveled often with a group of close friends. Ross loved to talk and enjoyed conversation. He was interested in people and could talk to anyone about anything and remember everything people said about themselves. Ross made people feel relaxed and welcome in social situations and was instantly liked by everyone he met.

On occasion, Carey would chide Ross, warning him to curtail his chatting when service people came to the house. She knew if she left him to his own devices, she would come home hours later and find the service person drinking beer with Ross—and staying for dinner. At other times, Ross would run out to the garage to get something and not come back for hours. Inevitably, he saw a neighbor when he opened the door and would start chatting. Then he would wander down the street talking to more neighbors. Carey often joked with him that if he disappeared, she would have a hard time finding him among so many friends and neighbors.

Carey and Ross also shared many lighthearted moments together. Ross knew Carey's favorite beverage was Diet Coke, and he also knew she wanted it in a cup with ice and a straw. Every time they stopped at a convenience store for drinks, he prepared her Diet Coke just how she liked it. Then he pretended to trip in front of the car when he came outside, threatening to fall and spill the drink—every time for thirty years. She was sure that in one of those instances, he would actually face-plant, and if he did, she would not be able to stop herself from laughing.

Seven years into their marriage, Carey and Ross had a son, Cole. Two years later, a girl, Laurel, was born. Carey had worked for several employers, but she set out on her own as an entrepreneur while pregnant with Laurel. This gave Carey the best of both worlds—having her own home-based business with a flexible schedule that allowed her time with the children.

Life was great, and Carey and Ross were able to provide a good home and consistent lifestyle for their family. The house they lived in when the kids were little had a red door and a huge backyard with a trampoline. The house with the red door soon became the neighborhood "Kool-Aid house," where all the kids wanted to play. Cole, Laurel, and their friends also enjoyed a finished basement with a pool and Ping-Pong table. Both childhood havens, the trampoline and the basement, provided countless memories of carefree fun.

Cole and Laurel had a close bond and did everything together, playing for hours and making up countless games. In grade school, they made a house out of a refrigerator box and lived in it for a week, talking, watching TV, eating Bugles snacks, and reading books. Cole adored his sister, and at times, they even acted like an old married couple. They talked constantly (actually she talked, and he listened). They made up games, laughed, and were best buds at every stage of their childhoods—even through some phases of sibling rivalry and bickering. Cole thought the world of his little sister and let her know it all the time. He also loved having a full house of people and making memories with his family and friends.

As they got older, Cole and Laurel's creativity evolved. They wrote and performed skits that Cole videotaped. One night, Laurel dressed up like an old woman, and Cole donned a wild rock-star wig that stuck out like he had been electrocuted. They taped their legs with duct tape, calves to thighs, and attached shoes to their knee-caps, which made them look like comical, miniature adults. Ross lifted them onto the Ping-Pong table and videotaped them as they tried to play the game. Everyone laughed until they cried.

Both kids were also active in sports, supported by Mom and Dad. Cole loved golf, skiing, deep-sea fishing, fly-fishing, and tennis, which he played at the collegiate level. Laurel thrived in almost any sport. When she tried to keep up with her big brother on the ski slopes,

Cole pushed her to go the extra mile and be tougher than any of the boys—mainly so they wouldn't date her. They also loved to camp with their dad, an Eagle Scout. One of Ross's favorite activities was to take the kids and their friends camping and teach them survival skills, such as how to gut a fish and take a bath in a lake of melted snow.

Cole and Laurel went to a private Christian school run by their church. The whole family was heavily involved with activities and families in the church, including yearly church retreats. Laurel even taught Sunday school with her dad.

Cole eventually went to Colorado State University to pursue a career in communications and was involved in fraternity life and leadership on campus. Following in her parents' footsteps, Laurel went to Oklahoma State University, but being separated from her family was a great challenge for her. On the other hand, the college experience deepened her bond with her dad, as father and daughter, student and alumnus, and die-hard Oklahoma State Cowboys fans.

Even as a child, Laurel appreciated how wonderful her family was. Some of her friends' families had been torn apart by divorce, and some had even lost a parent. Her life was consistent and stable, and others felt it too. They were a model family—until everything changed.

Like every family, the Conleys had to deal with the small and large stresses of school, careers, and family life. For a long time, Ross had been very successful in his sales career. He was revered and respected by all who interacted with him, and many of his colleagues became good friends. His work situation began to change about the time the kids went to college. A merger was imminent, and he became anxious about what that would mean for him. He took his role as provider and protector of his family very seriously and worried if he would still have a job. Carey spent hours almost every night talking the situation through with him, reassuring him they were financially stable and that everything would be fine.

At the same time, the couple was confronting other challenges, including becoming empty nesters who were struggling to find a new path together as a couple. Laurel also had some concerns that her parents were having marital problems, but she thought they would be able to work through their rough spot, and things would be fine. Ross and Carey also had hope they would figure it out.

But Ross was becoming a different person. He no longer wanted to go out and socialize, and Carey often felt like he was "not there" when they were together. In addition, they both worried incessantly about Cole when he took a five-week trip to Asia by himself. Carey was concerned that all the stress on Ross would lead to a heart attack. The morning after Cole came home safely from his Asia trip, Ross got up early, showered, and left the house. Carey found a note saying that he had gone to a meeting. She got excited, thinking that he was getting out, talking to people again, and taking steps toward deciding what he could do about his career.

Later that day, Carey was out working when she received an urgent message from the police. They had news about her husband but would not tell her anything about it over the phone. She knew something was seriously wrong and drove home immediately. The police were there and had given Cole the news.

Ross had driven to a reservoir, parked his car, and shot himself.

The Conley family's world shattered the day Ross died.

Just the day before, Laurel had been having a great summer at college. She had been excited about seeing friends, her summer school class, and her brother coming home safely from Asia.

Then she got a call from Cole: "Dad took his life this morning."

In shock, Laurel got up and punched a hole through a window. Her hand was bleeding, and shards of glass lay everywhere. She knew she had to get home immediately but did not want to go alone. She called one of her best friends, who had lost her dad two months previous-ly, for help. Laurel thought she would know what to do and would take her home. Other friends helped too. One of her roommates packed a bag for her, and her other roommate put her in the shower.

Once home, Laurel talked with her mom and Cole, trying to understand what had happened. Everything was occurring in a haze—conversations, people coming and going from the house. That night, she tried to sleep but every time she drifted off, she startled awake in a panic.

The next day, she went with Cole to the police station to identify her dad's belongings. They gave her a bag that contained his wedding ring, wallet, black comb—and a bullet. She freaked out, screaming, "I don't want it! Why would you give that to me?"

They told her they were required to give her every-thing that was on her father's person at the time of his death. A police officer then described what had happened. She listened, thinking she needed to hear everything to understand the reality of it. The officer told her that her father was found in an immaculate car, showered and in fresh, clean clothes. When she and Cole left the police station, she was in shock and stumbled and fell in the parking lot. Cole helped her up, looked her straight in the eye, and said, "I promise I will never do this to you."

After his father's death, Cole started his first job after

college, working in video production for an Arizona TV station. Despite his grief, he was able to find some joy in his job, excelling in his role on the station's social media team. His creativity, vision, and eye for bringing things to life served him well behind the camera, and he was promoted twice into high-profile positions. At the same time, the demands of work became extremely stressful, including long hours at a computer screen. He also struggled to adjust to post-college life. Cole was introspective and creative, but he loved spending time with friends. He had had many friends in college, and he worked hard at making new friends at work, but it did not happen as easily or quickly as it had at school. He was also trying to figure out his path in life beyond working at the television station. All these elements increased his stress, and he became more and more anxious.

About that time, Laurel, her boyfriend, Ethan, and some friends planned a trip to meet up with Cole in Austin, Texas. During the trip, Laurel noticed that something wasn't right with Cole. He was not acting like his usual self, and he was quiet and withdrawn. He seemed to be physically distancing himself from Laurel, so she decided to visit him soon at his place in Arizona. She had a feeling he needed her to be with him, and she thought that once she got there, everything would be fine.

Cole's life was unraveling more than anyone suspected.

He was stressed from his job and the challenges in making new friends. He questioned who he was and what he was doing. He told his mother he thought he had "blown it" and believed he had made all the wrong decisions, including buying his condo and car. He said he felt lost and didn't know what he was going to do with the rest of his life.

He knew he needed to leave his high-stress job, but the idea of quitting a good position was difficult for him to accept—as it had been for his father. Carey encouraged him to take some time off. He agreed to talk about it with his boss. Carey texted him later that day to hear how the discussion went, but he never answered her text. She got worried and drove to his condo. Finally, he called her back; he was at her house in Arizona. He had had the meeting and had told his boss he needed time off. Despite that, Carey was concerned, so she took him to see a counselor that night. They began sorting things out, and he made the decision to leave his job altogether. He planned to meet again with his boss the next day to tell him.

The next morning, Cole drove with Carey downtown so she could attend a luncheon while he met with his boss. He was anxious and fidgety but assured Carey that once he got through the meeting, everything would be fine. He agreed to return to pick her up after the meeting, but he never showed up. Instead of attending the meeting with his boss, he had panicked and gone back to his condo. When he didn't answer any of Carey's calls and texts, she called the police then a family member to pick her up. When she arrived at Cole's condo, the police had already arrived. Cole had died of a self-inflicted gunshot.

The deaths of Ross and Cole left the Conley family devastated and struggling to cope as they grappled with difficult questions. Why had this kind of tragedy happened? Should they have seen it coming?

Carey and Laurel's lives were forever altered, and to survive, they had to create new ways of living and perceiving life. They began to heal by making job decisions to allow flexibility to be together as often as they could, choosing positive relationships, putting their needs first, learning how to forgive, and embracing new identities. They also had to confront their misconceptions and learn new ways to find help and support—and to become support for each other. Eventually, they moved from loss and grief to eternal gain, finding heaven on Earth. What they learned is the hope they want to give to you.

CHAPTER 1

Leaving Planet Normal

After Ross's death, Carey and Laurel's lives blew up. In a split second, everything they knew and thought was normal was shattered. It's hard to define the experience to those who have not had that level of tragedy, but it was like being trapped on a rocket ship. Ross's death blasted them from their world. Then, with Cole's death, the rocket boosters disengaged, and Carey and Laurel found themselves in orbit in a totally different sphere. They were hijacked from Planet Normal and thrust into an alien world. They had to function in *this* world, but their hearts and minds remained in a completely different place.

CAREY

Before this happened to our family, we didn't understand people who had experienced tragedy, because we hadn't lived it ourselves. Our extended family and large community of friends and acquaintances thought we "had it all." They pictured us as the beautiful, successful image of the American family—what every family dreams of being. We lived in a bubble and were not completely aware of it. We had successful careers, a strong faith, and loving family relationships. Our world was one of nice homes and families that appeared "put together." We all sent our kids to the best schools and were active in all their activities.

Ross was a great husband. He was aware of all my likes and dislikes and acted on his intuition of what I needed. One of the first things I loved about him was his magnetic presence in a room. People naturally gravitated to him, and because of that, I knew we could go anywhere together and have a great time. He was also an amazing father to Cole and Laurel. He had a special relationship with them, and they truly enjoyed being with him. He was more than their father: he was their mentor and friend. I knew he loved us all very much and would always take care of us. Before he died by suicide, he ensured we would be all right, leaving money and keys for us, although no note.

Looking back, I remember having unsettling feelings the few weeks before his death.

My son, Cole, was pure joy. From the moment he was born, he brought happiness to everyone. He was easygoing and introspective. His quiet nature made him intuitive and sensitive to other people's feelings, and he silently helped many friends and family members through their struggles. He also had a way of putting people at ease and making them laugh, lighting up many people's lives. He loved many things: beautiful scenery, sunsets, warm weather, music, exploring new places, golf, and showing people around Arizona, his home state after college.

One year when we returned from a Christmas cruise together, we heard that two kids who went to high school with Laurel and Cole had committed suicide over the holidays. As a family, we discussed how unbelievably selfish it was for someone to take his or her own life. We didn't understand then what we do now. We couldn't understand how anyone could make a decision that would cause so much pain to others and forever impact their friends and family.

We never expected suicide to happen in our family—not in a million years. No one in our extended family or community expected it either. We believed everyone struggled with hard times in their lives and that problems generally worked themselves out. We didn't know what we didn't know. When we were thrown into a world in which problems didn't work themselves out, our perspective changed drastically.

Warning signs or risks for suicide, such as depression or addiction problems, may not always be obvious. In our family's case, we knew Ross and Cole had been going through rough times, but they did not have typical signs of mental illness, and we never thought they were suicidal. Would you suspect that loved ones would consider taking their life just because they were feeling down or confused? No one ever wants to see that coming.

Before my husband's and son's deaths, many of our friends and family members did not tell us about their tragedies and their experiences with loss and grief. Once they heard our story, they opened up and shared theirs with us. I have discovered that no one is "normal." Even so-called "model" families aren't perfect and have underlying struggles about which people outside the household are unaware. Everyone has a story, and no one lives on Planet Normal.

LAUREL

After the deaths of my father and brother, I kept hoping to find "normal" again, but I no longer knew what that was. For the first twenty years of my life, I had lived a life many others did not find "normal." I didn't realize other people thought of our family as different. Some might even have thought our family was nearly perfect. Looking back, I realize that those two decades of my life were close to perfect for me.

I was born into a loving family that consisted of my older brother, who was two at the time, and my parents. I was raised in the beautiful state of Colorado where the mountains were always a short drive away and the seasons were almost storybook ideal. The first home I lived in had a large backyard, and family and friends flowed in and out with the many celebrations and dinner parties we hosted. My relationship with my brother was closer than most. We had our periods of bickering, but we never stayed mad at each other for long. My dad was a huge encourager and my go-to guy for answers. We could talk for hours about anything without an end in sight. He was also my toughest critic—and he taught me the hardest lessons. My dad had lost his own brother when I was only three years old. If Cole and I were ever arguing, he would say, "At least you have each other." That phrase always reminded me to be thankful for what I have and to not take that for granted.

Our home was stable, and our family was close. The only major changes I experienced in my early years were playing multiple sports (I never quite found my niche) and constantly redecorating my bedroom. I believed all families were like we were.

In college, I got my first insight into how different families could be. It happened the night I participated in a sorority circle called "truth night," which required the sorority sisters to share their upbringing and family stories. The goal was to help us bond, but I was surprised to learn how much some of their families had struggled and about the trauma some had faced at a young age. I didn't know what to say, and I felt guilty about my "normal" life.

After my dad's and Cole's deaths, I was plunged into a different world and was forced to create a new normal for myself. I struggled with even the simplest everyday routines and tasks I had taken for granted, such as sleeping securely and soundly in my own bedroom. I took to spending the night on the couch because nothing felt right in my life. Even my own room couldn't bring me comfort. I felt so out of sorts and was barely sleeping. One night after spending the night on the couch in the living room, I woke up believing that the suicides had all been just a bad dream. For a few glorious moments, my dad and brother were still alive. Relief flooded through me, but the feeling passed quickly, and the reality of what had happened sucker-punched me in the gut.

Today, I see and understand more of the pain and struggles that affect others. Before my father's and brother's deaths, people did not tell me about their adversities because they knew I would not understand. I had not experienced anything like the kind of problems they were dealing with, so what could I have possibly said or done to help them? Now they know I can relate.

REFLECTIONS AND QUESTIONS TO CONSIDER

No matter how blessed or "normal" a family appears, they all have good times and hard times and experience loss and grief. Here are some ideas to help you relate to the struggles of others. You can also discuss them within your family and circles of friends to help build relationships in which everyone feels comfortable sharing their stories and feelings about their struggles and successes.

- What big or small experiences of loss or adversity in your personal or family life can help you understand the pain and struggles of others?

- You feel most comfortable sharing your story of loss or adversity with someone who has experienced . . .

- How do you think others view you and your family? How do you see other people and their families?

CHAPTER 2

Shock and Exhaustion

In the first few days after the deaths of Ross and Cole, Carey and Laurel were in a state of physical, emotional, and mental shock. It was surreal—unreal. They couldn't believe it. There was no time to absorb and recover from the shock, and they were forced to deal immediately with the reality of the deaths.

CAREY

When Ross died so unexpectedly, I was faced with many tough decisions to make in a short time. I had to find a funeral home and have his body sent there within forty-eight hours of his death. There were exhaustive piles of paperwork to sign, and we had to answer painful and horrible questions from the mortician and the police.

While trying to deal with that, a voice in my head kept screaming that this horrible thing hadn't happened at all. I kept expecting Ross to walk through the door. My mind played tricks on me because I had been accustomed to living life a certain way for so long. At the same time, I was waking up every morning and reliving the whole tragedy in my mind. I replayed it over and over again.

The shock and grief were exhausting, and we were stressed by the many decisions and tasks suddenly forced on us. The simple act of taking care of ourselves became overwhelming, and we could not think clearly through the details of every decision and interaction. We were existing outside ourselves and trying to survive moment by moment. Unfortunately, we fear we hurt some people by not being emotionally "up" and able to support them. We were in so much pain that we did not understand the pain others were in and how much they needed to grieve too.

LAUREL

For the first few weeks after my dad's death, I replayed in my mind the agonizing information the police officer had told me. Reliving his last moment exhausted me emotionally, but I had to do it to try to understand what had happened and make sense of it.

Two days after Dad died, there were still a lot of people we had to tell, but I was so emotionally exhausted at that point I no longer had the energy left to share in their feelings. I sat there while they cried and I waited for their tears to pass. I felt bad because I wanted to comfort them, but I just couldn't do it anymore. I knew that the loss of my dad affected more than just me, but I was so wrung out, I didn't have anything left to offer someone else.

After my dad's service, we were inundated at the reception by well-meaning people who engulfed me with hugs. Overwhelmed by the massive outpouring of emotion, I went into an anxiety-fueled tailspin that triggered a panic attack. I was terrified because I had never had a panic attack before, and it took me some time to realize what was happening to my body. I had to shut myself up in the bathroom to recover.

I had not experienced intense situations before my dad passed, so it was a process for me to learn and understand how I reacted in times of distress. The initial few days after his loss seemed like a whirlwind, and I was barely making it to the next moment.

After that experience with my dad's reception, when Cole died, we decided to have a private reception for him at a later time after the funeral, which gave us a few hours to rest before facing the masses. Still, I braced myself for the onslaught of attention and emotions I knew would come. I flipped the switch to "defensive mode" until the reception was over and avoided another panic attack, but I was numb from shock and exhaustion. Despite this, I was more understanding and patient with myself and had learned to trust my gut and give myself what I needed, which made all the difference.

REFLECTIONS AND QUESTIONS TO CONSIDER

Tragedy can produce crushing shock and exhaustion for those closest to it. Here are some ideas to help you understand and best support someone who is facing devastating loss and grief. You can also discuss these points within your family and circles of friends to understand the best way to help each other during times of extreme duress.

- What would help you minimize exhaustion when experiencing tragedy or a loss?

- Are you a people pleaser? If so, what can others do to minimize your anxiety about not pleasing everyone when you experience loss and grief?

- Who are the people pleasers in your family and circles of friends? What can you do to help them

minimize their anxiety about not pleasing everyone when they experience loss and grief?

- Think about the types of things or actions that
  bring you the most comfort. How might those
  things help you when experiencing tragedy or a
  loss?

- How do you prefer to be comforted? For example, do you prefer hugs or talking?

CHAPTER 3

Preparing for Impact:

MUSTERING YOUR SUPER-SAFE PEOPLE

The instant people hear there is a death in a family, they often flood the family's home, all wanting to be there at the same time. However, an onslaught of friends, acquaintances, and extended family can be overwhelming and make things more difficult for those who are grieving.

CAREY

We were involved in a big church and school community, and after Ross's death, we were overwhelmed by well-intentioned people who wanted to console us and offer help. The numbers quickly became too much to deal with, and we had to scramble to put up gates to protect ourselves. We were reeling from the shock and desperate for privacy and much-needed rest. Unfortunately, some people did not understand why we locked them out. Feelings were hurt, and we lost some relationships because of it.

After Cole's death, we knew what would happen, so we immediately put a process in place, releasing information in a controlled way that allowed us to prepare for the impact of it. We told a handful of key people in our lives right away. We chose a few we could trust to protect us and keep things under wraps until we were ready to go public. We also knew those people would not push their own emotions on us and would help us in the ways we needed. We called them our super-safe people. They had been our friends for a long time, and to this day, they have never asked us to tell the story of Ross's and Cole's deaths, and they never would. They respect and love us without needing to know any more details beyond what we choose to share.

We waited forty-eight hours to tell people outside that super-safe circle and before posting an announcement on social media. We felt as if we had to build a moat around the house with a drawbridge and a gatekeeper. I chose a super-safe person to become the gatekeeper, someone I trusted to know who should cross the drawbridge and who shouldn't. That person conveyed information as directed by me, including what we needed for support and, most important, what we didn't need.

LAUREL

To defend myself emotionally, I had not let myself cry much after my brother's death. When I finally allowed myself to be upset and sob, my best friend sat across from me, allowing me to release my emotion without touching me. She let me know that she was there for me, but as much as she wanted to hug me in that moment, she knew that was not what I needed. She was my super-safe person. We later laughed about how people had been overwhelmingly trying to hug me, and I thanked her for refraining from it in that moment.

She let me cry as long as I wanted without trying to force me to feel better before I was ready. When I was done, we went to Target and blew $250 buying random stuff. She understood I had needed to have her near me while I cried and sensed that she should take me to do something lighthearted, like the Target shopping sprees we had frequently done together in high school. She knew that having some fun in a familiar place where no one knew what had happened would be therapeutic for me.

If you experience a loss or adversity and feel overwhelmed by people, go with your gut when choosing your super-safe people. My gut told me that my super-safe people would be those with whom I felt one-hundred percent comfortable talking about anything—or nothing. I found that I felt anxious when I thought about doing that with certain people. I had to be decisive about who the safe people were for me and separate myself from those who weren't—and not feel guilty about it.

Just after the death of my dad, I assumed that certain people would be my super-safe people and support system. Sometimes I was disappointed. I thought I knew people, but it's amazing what I have learned about relationships through this experience. There are friends and family members who will text and stay in touch for the first two weeks before going back to their normal lives and concerns, which is understandable. I call them the two-week texters. Their intentions were sincere, but they later unintentionally left me feeling abandoned. Over time, I recognized that the people who were still reaching out to me months and years later were my super-safe people. They are the ones who understand that my pain and grief did not disappear after a couple of weeks.

You might be surprised to find your super-safe people are not the ones you thought they would be, and others you hadn't thought of become your most reliable support. Be open-minded to accepting those you would not have expected. It's important to give others a chance to become those special people for you.

REFLECTIONS AND QUESTIONS TO CONSIDER

Someone suffering a tragic loss needs to be surrounded by people who best understand how to support them emotionally and protect them from people who don't. Here are some ideas to help you be that super-safe person for someone. You can also discuss these points within your family and circles of friends to learn how to become a super-safe group of people for each other.

- What do you need most when you are facing a loss or struggling with a tough time? Do you prefer time alone or do you want to be surrounded by people at all times? Do you need a little of both?

- Consider how you would set up boundaries to protect yourself during a tragedy. For example, would you set specific hours to visit with friends? Would you turn off your phone for certain periods of time?

- Who would you first turn to when faced with tragedy or serious loss? Take a look at your circle of family and friends and ask yourself who would respect you and prioritize your needs in a time of adversity. Think about what qualities would make someone a safe person in your life.

- Consider the people in your life for whom you would be a super-safe person.

- Ask a grieving person to help you understand what he or she needs the most. Does that person need to cry or not to cry? What types of activity would help the most?

- Who can you reach out to today? Think of someone you know who has experienced tragedy a while ago and reach out to them.

CHAPTER 4

Becoming a Story

The Conleys soon discovered that their family had become a "story." After Ross's death, they were no longer Carey, Laurel, and Cole; they were a tragedy. They were no longer seen as individuals in a family. They felt they could not be themselves among others, which drastically changed how they interacted within their extended family and community.

CAREY

I couldn't even go for a walk in my own neighborhood without feeling my neighbors' pitiful looks. I know they felt for us and were trying to empathize, but every time I saw their expressions, I had to relive the tragedy. Every time we were asked about what had happened, we relived it again as that person experienced the shock and pain of it themselves for the first time.

We almost had to isolate ourselves because everywhere we would normally go, we knew someone or someone knew us. We would get the woeful looks or worse, the insensitive questions, such as, "Did you see it coming?" In one case, I was walking outside a restaurant past the patio, and a woman I barely knew jumped out of her chair, grabbed me, and bombarded me with questions. Some people don't understand when they cross the line. They might be trying to sympathize, but they can't empathize, often because they haven't been through something similar. I soon could sense when someone was going to press us inappropriately for details or ask prying questions, and I learned to shut it down quickly.

When you sense people are going too far, or when they are making you feel uncomfortable about a loss or adversity you have experienced, do not feel pressured to engage with them, even if you know them well. You do not have to tolerate it. The best course of action is to shut down the conversation quickly and politely excuse yourself.

If you want to support someone who has experienced loss or tragedy, understand that you don't need to know everything. Accept the information that is released by the immediate family without asking more questions, which can cause them more anguish.

LAUREL

People who have never experienced a tragedy might not understand that they don't need to know all the details of someone else's tragedy. They might ask intrusive questions because they feel like they *should* be asking, or because they are prying but pretending they are concerned, or because they're simply making conversation.

I work at an event venue and once had to coordinate a funeral for a family who had lost their daughter. I was glad I was in charge of it because I knew exactly how they felt. When my mom had planned Cole's funeral, the event planner had asked many unnecessary, personal questions, causing her more pain. As that family sat in my office, I did not ask them any questions about their daughter's death because I understood how tired they were of talking about it and knew the distress that caused them. I knew the family needed me to help them with the planning and make them comfortable, which meant giving them a break from answering questions.

People outside the immediate circle of a loss or tragedy often want to understand what has happened and why. They might also be curious or feel like they need to say something, but there is a point at which you don't need to say or ask anything.

REFLECTIONS AND QUESTIONS TO CONSIDER

Tragedy can attract a lot of inappropriate attention and put a person or family in an unwanted spotlight, which can cause more stress and pain. Here are some ideas to help you set boundaries for the amount of sharing you want to do when you are struggling with loss or a traumatic situation. You can also discuss these points within your family and circles of friends to learn how to support and protect each other from unwanted attention when experiencing adversity or loss.

- How many intimate details of your personal life do you normally like sharing with close friends and family?

- How many intimate details of your personal life do you normally like sharing with acquaintances or more distant relatives?

- How free are you in sharing intimate or personal stories with people you barely know?

- Have you ever told someone that something is none of their business?

- With your super-safe person or group, practice telling each other statements like these:

  - "I would prefer not to talk about something so painful for me."

  - "I don't want to talk about it."

  - "I would rather talk about something else."

CHAPTER 5

Mirroring the Needs of Someone Who Grieves

When someone experiences a tragic loss, friends and family want to be supportive and often feel the need to do something active to help. Their hearts may be in the right place, but some of the traditional ways to help, such as bringing food, aren't always what the family needs most. In addition, people might offer clichés or pat advice that do not work for every individual and situation. The best way to help others in a time of loss is by mirroring their needs and behaviors.

CAREY

After the deaths of Ross and Cole, people offered us a lot of food and many hugs. These things were helpful and much appreciated, but we needed other things too, such as rides to and from the airport. I also needed someone to stay in my house and take care of our dog when I was gone. One good friend did that for me, another friend assisted us with the financial side of things, and another found the right mortician. These things were extremely helpful and reduced our stress tremendously.

We received a lot of advice from friends and family about how to handle our grieving and healing processes. For example, I was flooded with recommendations for self-help books and grief support groups—and I am *so* not that girl. I was also told many times not to make any big life changes or financial decisions in the first year after Ross's death, such as selling the house and moving. However, I no longer wanted to be in Denver. I needed to be free to be with Laurel at a moment's notice and to be near Cole in Arizona as he started his new job. In addition, because no one knew me in Arizona, I wasn't a "story" there. It was a safe place away from constant attention, which helped me rest and avoid the exhaustion of reliving the death over and over every time I saw people I knew in Colorado.

Although well-meaning, the advice not to make big decisions was not going to work for me, so I moved, at first part time, to Arizona to be near Cole. I eventually sold the house in Colorado and moved to Arizona permanently. That was the best course of action for me.

Because we are a Christian family, people in our congregation wanted to ensure we got Christian counseling and stayed with the church after Ross's death. They were praying hard for us, and many got worried about our relationships with God when they hadn't seen us in church for a while. Because we had so many family memories at that church, it was too painful for us to go back there. We just couldn't do it. For a time, I was also angry with God and had separated from my conversations with Him.

Eventually, I started going to a new church with Cole in Arizona. Then after Cole died, I stopped going again and have not been back. My decision to leave the church really bothered some people, but they didn't understand I had to move inward to rebuild my relationship with God. At the end of the day, God and I had to get through it together. Now our relationship is stronger than it has ever been.

No matter what your faith or spiritual beliefs are, it's important to honor them in the way that is right for you. It's just as important to honor the beliefs of others and the way they choose to practice—or not practice—when they are mourning. Try to understand that someone does not have to publicly practice their faith or spirituality, or approach it in the way they once did, to have a relationship with God or stay in touch with their beliefs.

The way in which one person chooses to grieve and heal might not be the best way for someone else. It is different for everybody. Allow people to handle their processes in the way they choose. Instead of offering canned advice and projecting expectations, follow his or her lead and mirror their behavior. For example, if I wanted to laugh, my super-safe people would laugh with me. If I wanted to cry, they let me cry and maybe cried too. If I needed quiet time without talking, they were fine with that. If I wanted to talk about Cole or Ross and share funny stories, they joined me in the discussion with their own memories.

Mirroring the behavior of someone who is grieving is a beautiful gift you can give. We love it when people talk about Ross and Cole in a positive way and share good memories. That helps keep them alive for us. I am sad when people don't engage with me when I want to talk about them.

Death makes some people want to circle up others to hug and cry together. When people wanted that from us and we couldn't offer it, it was hard for them to accept, especially because it is expected funeral behavior. We followed some expected behaviors and traditions at Ross's funeral but decided to do what was best for us at Cole's. For example, we chose not to stand and receive a line of hundreds of people who wanted to hug us.

When loss or tragedy happens to friends or family members, remember that it's not about protocol, tradition, or doctrine, and it's not about you. If you truly want to help, support the decisions they make and respect their need to handle their loss and healing in their own way without adding expectations, judgment, or unconstructive advice.

LAUREL

I didn't realize right away what I needed the most after I lost my father and brother, but the best help came from people who were thoughtful in their support. Some friends bought us restaurant gift cards, which gave us the ability to feed people staying with us at any time. Other people offered to pick up people coming from out of town at the airport. In another case, a friend who worked for a valet service sent a free SUV to take us to the funeral, so we didn't have to worry about driving and parking. Thoughtful gestures like that were so helpful because they saved us from having to think through and plan every detail.

When I was with my safe people after the deaths of my dad and brother, I just wanted to talk everything out and get it all out there. I'm an external processor who has to talk through everything. On the other hand, my mom is an internal processor, so when people wanted to talk to her about the deaths, she ran out of words. My safe people accepted the way in which I needed to process things on my own terms, but not everybody understood that.

Sometimes people who have experienced a loss feel pressured to exhibit their emotions and grief in expected ways, such as speaking at the funeral or service of a loved one. After my dad died, I was so overwhelmed and in such shock, I could not have possibly spoken at the service. I agonized over making the decision not to speak, but my closest friend stepped up to speak on my behalf at my dad's funeral. It was beyond selfless and is something I will never forget. She was strong for me when I couldn't bring myself to speak.

When Cole died, I was older, more mature, and had been through the experience before. My dad's death had made me a different person, so when my brother died, I felt like it was my duty to speak on his behalf. I do not regret either of those decisions about speaking.

My now-husband, Ethan, and I were dating when Cole died. Ethan had gotten to know Cole and had become a close friend of his. He suffered almost as much shock and emotional trauma as we did, so I helped navigate the situation for him. I had to be there as much for him as he was for me. Having that experience together brought us closer, and I'm grateful for that. We had already been talking about getting engaged just before Cole died and decided to move forward with our plans exactly one month after his death. I struggled with how our engagement was going to be perceived so soon after the tragedy. I was concerned people might think I was disregarding our family's loss and moving right into wedding mode. Looking back, I now see that was what we needed to focus on at the time. It was also what Cole would have wanted us to do.

In a time of tragedy and loss, you have to do what is best for yourself and not feel guilty about it. If people are demanding your time when you need time to yourself, say no. If people are judging your decisions or telling you what you should or shouldn't do, do not feel pressured to do things their way. It's OK to make decisions that may appear unwise or selfish to others because your life after loss is not about them; you have to live it yourself. The journey from grieving to healing is tough, and you have to navigate the waters in your own way and at your own pace.

If you know someone who is grieving, ask the person what would help the most. Before offering advice, take a moment to put yourself in his or her shoes and try to understand and support their decisions.

REFLECTIONS AND QUESTIONS TO CONSIDER

People suffering loss and adversity need all kinds of help—in little and big ways. Needs can vary a lot among individuals and families. Everyone grieves in their own way, and the manner in which they react or behave might or might not be what you expect. Here are some ideas to help you respect the unique ways others grieve so you can put their healing first and not make it about you. You can also discuss these points within your family and circles of friends to learn the best way to help each other.

- What kinds of things most help you when you are facing extreme challenges or hard times? Would you desperately need childcare? Would you really appreciate for someone knowledgeable about cars to take your car to the mechanic? Would picking up groceries or mowing your lawn take some stress off your plate?

- When a friend or family member is grieving or struggling with challenges, ask them what you can do that would help the most. Consider who they are and their lifestyle and offer thoughtful suggestions. For example, ask if it would help for you to walk the dog, pick up their kids at school, or run errands.

- When a friend or family member is having challenges or suffers a loss, do you assume you know how they should handle things?

- Are you forcing others to deal with new life circumstances as you would expect to, or are you truly putting them first and respecting their ideas?

- With your super-safe person or group, practice telling each other statements like these:

  - "What do you need most from me as your friend/loved one?"

  - "The thing I need most from you as my friend/loved one is to let me ... ."

  - "What do you think is the best thing for you to do now?"

  - "The best thing for me to do now is ... ."

CHAPTER 6

Establishing a New Identity

Losing loved ones can leave holes in our lives no one else can fill. These holes affect our identities. Redefining your identity after loss can be like riding a teeter-totter between who you were and who you will become. How people perceived you can make it difficult for you to adjust to the new roles and the new self you will need to develop. You may no longer serve the family in the way you had. In addition, your interests may change, and friendships can dissipate because you no longer fit in socially or have the same things in common.

CAREY

When Ross died, a friend told me that my identity was going to change. I knew the obvious thing was going to change—no longer wife, now called widow. What I didn't realize was how deeply it would impact me and my personality.

One morning not long ago, I was cleaning my apartment and making lists while listening to Pandora. I was fully immersed in the moment as one of Ross's and my favorite songs began to play. I stopped dead in my tracks as I was transported back in time by "our song." In a split second, my identity shifted from who I was to who I had been. For several moments, it paralyzed me. Who was I, *really*?

As a society, we place so much emphasis on our roles, titles, and relationships with others to build our identities, that when those things change or disappear, we feel lost. I questioned how I was supposed to act and struggled to re-identify who I was. I had to go through a lot of soul searching to rediscover myself. Society does try to recognize how loss changes our identities by providing titles, such as "widow" for a woman who has lost her husband and "orphan" for a child who has lost parents. When I lost Cole, there was no title for me, a parent who has lost a child. Even if there were one, it would provide cold comfort. There are titles for loss but not for grief or its impact on someone's identity.

The first time I had to check the marital status box on a form after Ross's death, it took me five minutes to force myself to do it. Logically, I knew I was single, but my husband and I had been together since my junior year of high school, most of my life, and I still felt like his wife. So how was I to categorize myself in my own mind and on that piece of paper? I knew that I was no longer going to be "wife" or "Mrs." I had to accept that my new title was single or widow. Widow is a title I don't like, so I do not use it often, but I prefer it to single. Saying I'm single implies I am on the market and looking for a relationship. When I say I am a widow, people don't make that assumption, although both terms are labels and I get reactions either way.

Worst of all, losing my son robbed me of hearing my son call me Mom. I had a vision of being mother of the groom, having a daughter-in-law to love, and grandchildren who would look like my son. When the roles and titles of wife and a son's mother were taken from me, some of my personality shifted. I began to see how we place our identities in titles and the parts we play in our families and communities; we attach our identities to other people to complete ourselves.

Consider the empty nest syndrome. This was a hard time for Ross and me as well, as we were rediscovering who we were, as individuals and as a married couple.

Parents sometimes struggle with defining new identities and with their relationships to each other after their kids go off to college. They have attached so much of their identities to their children, they feel lost once they are gone. It can be difficult for parents to let go and find new ways to spend their time in their empty nest. This can be hard on the marriage as well, especially if a married couple hasn't spent time developing their relationship as its own entity. The couple can easily drift apart as the children grow and suddenly realize once they are gone that they have nothing left in common. At that point, it is very hard to try and find thing to enjoy together. Couples who sail successfully through empty nest syndrome tend to have made the effort to enjoy things together throughout the years.

My role in my surviving family also changed, as did family relationships. I had played a part in keeping the extended family connected and getting us together, but that responsibility shifted more to others after Ross died. It was difficult to lose that position within the extended family, and I did not know how to act anymore at family functions. Although I had made the logistical arrangements for family gatherings, my husband had been the talker who made sure everyone in the family was comfortable within the group. His absence left a gaping hole in family dynamics, and we felt awkward without him.

The first Christmas was stressful because no one knew how to deal with Laurel, Cole, and me in our new roles, which we were also trying to define and adjust to. The holes left by Ross's absence were obvious, and we were all unsure how to act and what we should and should not say. We had traditions in the family we tried to maintain, but it was never going to be the same, and we felt as if we were going through the motions.

My role in Laurel's life also changed. We are still mother and daughter, but we have developed a new bond with our evolving identities. She has had to grow up fast, and we have had to lean on each other for strength. In the process, we have become colleagues in carrying out to the world our mission and message of hope after loss. One of our projects together was writing this book.

I also had to learn not to expect Laurel to be the person Cole was. Laurel is different from Cole, with her own personality and special brand of love to offer. We have both learned this lesson: We are who we are. We are both unique and special and respect that we can't fill the roles of the people we have lost. As a result, we have grown in our relationship for each other. For example, Laurel considers long periods of talking with someone to be quality time. On the other hand, I have never been a "visitor" or a chit-chatter. I didn't need to have people circled around me just for the purpose of visiting. I get impatient with that. However, I try now to have more casual conversations with Laurel without feeling the need to have a specific or intentional reason to talk.

My role within friendships and social situations has also changed. Much of our social life and many of our friendships had revolved around other couples and their families. I still get invited to many social events, and I do attend events that involve women and mixed groups of people. However, I often decline events that involve only couples. At that kind of get-together, I feel like people are looking at me wondering, "Why is she single?" and "When is she going to be dating?" I can see the question marks over their heads and the gears turning in their minds: "I know the perfect guy to fix her up with."

After the loss of Ross and Cole, I wanted to be the same person and enjoy the same things, but I didn't anymore. I beat myself up about it and tried to convince myself that I could still go out and have fun. I forced myself to try to be that person. I soon realized that many social situations I used to enjoy didn't feel right and I no longer belonged there. I used to love being around a lot of people, and now it drains me quickly. For example, I once forced myself to attend a happy hour with some friends after Ross's death. After an hour, I found I was done, out of words, and had had enough. I told everyone I was tired and left. It was fun, but when Ross was still alive, he and I would have been the last to leave.

I began to see that I was not as extroverted as I once was. It takes a lot to get me to a party now, and I don't stay long. I am happier spending time with my small circle of super-safe people instead of spending lots of time with a large group of acquaintances. I protect my time and with whom I spend it now, and I didn't use to do that. My super-safe people give me a lot of grace and don't make me feel like I have to apologize or feel bad if I choose to leave early. They don't ask questions or expect anything from me; they just love me through it.

In addition, many of things I used to love no longer excite me the way they once did. I am currently searching out new interests I think may be a part of who I am to become as a person. I have started taking ballroom dancing classes, which I have always wanted to do. Ross and I had talked about dancing after the kids went to college, and we never did, so I bit the bullet and put on my dancing shoes. It has been fun and humbling as well, and I am glad I am trying new things.

My identity was also closely tied to our family home in Colorado, including all of its contents. Finding a new identity involved making some serious changes in the physical home we had loved so much. Laurel and I felt we needed to disconnect our identity from that physical space and from all the extraneous stuff owned by Ross,

Cole, and ourselves. People often place a lot of themselves into a home or other personal space and the things in it—which makes it extremely difficult to let them go when needed. Inevitably, the home owned by someone who has passed away will have to be purged of stuff. This can be very painful for those left behind, so I recommend slowly purging unnecessary clutter in your life and not leaving it for others.

After Ross's death, I chose to move away from Colorado, the state where I grew up, married, and raised my family for so many years. I no longer identified it as my home or the place I wanted to be. I didn't relate to the person I was there and felt I didn't belong there anymore. When I drive past our old house, I remember the wonderful memories and the history, but I can't identify with living there anymore.

LAUREL

The first twenty years of my life I shared with my dad and brother were blessed and joyful. I now believe having those good memories was God's way of preparing me to handle the new roles I would be forced to accept after their deaths. I lost a big part of my identity when I lost my dad and brother, and what remained was forever changed.

When my dad died, I was a twenty-year-old college student who had experienced two wonderful years at college. After the funeral, I returned to school as a very different person who viewed and interacted with the campus scene in a different way. I no longer identified with some of the friends and activities that used to bring me joy. I was hesitant to go on dates and get into relationships because I felt it wasn't fair to make someone else deal with the trauma I was going through. I also feared that I would never find someone who could handle it, so it was easier not to date than to be disappointed. It took some time, but as I started letting new people into my life, I began to figure out my identity as the daughter and sister of men who had committed suicide.

I met my husband, Ethan, six months after my dad's death, and the first time we hung out together, I unloaded the whole story on him. I told him I had to be honest about my baggage and would understand if he did not want to talk to me the next day. He ended up sticking around.

Opening the door to Ethan made me realize I could still share myself in an intimate relationship. I had identified as someone who carried a heavy burden others would not want to bear with me and did not realize how much people wanted to be a part of my life—baggage and all. That enlightening experience with Ethan made me see the kind of friend I was and could be, and I became a better friend to everyone because of it. I struggled to let go of the old me and allow myself to be vulnerable, but it had to be done.

Losing my father and brother at such a young age also changed my perspective and identity by forcing me to grow up fast. At only twenty years of age, many adult decisions and responsibilities landed in my lap, such as banking and finances, especially in relation to my tuition and college expenses. My dad had always taken care of these, and I instantly felt ten years older. My identity suddenly changed from college student to full-fledged adult—which I didn't want to be yet.

After my dad died, Cole stepped up and took on many of my dad's responsibilities. He felt he had to fill that role, yet he had to be himself, and I think he struggled with balancing that. Nonetheless, he was a big support for me at the time, and we grew closer because of it. After Cole died three years later, I faced a big adult decision about possibly uprooting my life and moving. By that time, I had graduated from college and had begun my adult working life in Oklahoma, but I felt as if I should not return there and considered moving to Arizona where my mom lived—just the two of us against the world. Moving to be physically closer to each other seemed like a good idea. However, because Cole had died in Arizona, I felt I had lost some of my identity in that state. Colorado was the state that represented my lost family life, so moving back there didn't feel right either. In the end, I chose to stay in Oklahoma where I had begun my new life and had already started to establish a new identity. It was the right thing to do for me.

The loss of my dad and brother also impacted my identity and the dynamics within our family. I believe I am the female version of my dad, sharing several physical attributes and personality traits. Imagine going through female puberty and realizing you are built like your dad! Good times. I am also a talker, just he was. We shared that identity and could talk together for hours. I had assumed that my mom shared that identity too, but after my dad died, I saw that she is more of a listener. I remember telling her, "Use more words." But I had to understand that the type of communication I had shared with my dad wasn't going to happen anymore. Over time, I found that sharing activities and projects with my mom gives us more to talk about. For example, we have had a great time working together writing this book.

Working together has also given us a positive diversion in the midst of a horrible time and has helped us develop new identities and roles in each other's lives. We have learned to work as a team and lean on each other when needed. We have also found we each have strengths that complement each other. Working together also provides a foundation to build communication with each other on a deep level. We now talk a lot and are planning more projects to work on together.

My dad also taught me that when I start a project, I finish it and give it my all. He stressed I should not take no for an answer if I am passionate about something. My husband recently joked that I don't like to hear "no," and I said, "You can thank Ross Conley for that."

I credit my ambition, determination, and killer work ethic to my dad. He was tenacious about getting what he wanted out of life, and he instilled that in me. He embodied the "work hard, play harder" slogan and taught me to problem-solve. When I went to him with a problem I thought was too big to handle on my own, he would often say, "Figure it out, Laurel." Without skipping a beat, he would repeat that parental phrase again and again, causing my adolescent eyes to roll. I wondered why he wouldn't jump in and save the day for me, but now I understand and am grateful for it. Whether I had to deal with a tough breakup, apply for college, or get my car serviced far away from home, I learned to figure it out. My dad gave me the space to learn by allowing me to make my own mistakes.

Because of my dad, I developed my independent and strong nature, and this is a big part of my identity to this day.

REFLECTIONS AND QUESTIONS TO CONSIDER

Your identity and the roles you play within your family and friendships, at work, and in your community can change after the death of someone close to you. You may no longer identify with some of your old friends, interests, or activities, or you may look toward others to fulfill the role a lost loved one once played in your life. You will need to allow yourself time to find ways to fill the gaps. When you are ready, slowly try new activities. Make new friendships, but don't expect someone else to become the person you have lost. Be OK with letting new people into your world and accept them as they are.

Developing a new identity takes time; you can't rush the process of filling the gap between who you were and who you will become. Give yourself all the space you need to allow your new identity and life to evolve. Here are some ideas to help you in the process. You can also discuss these points within your family and circles of friends to learn more about yourself as an individual beyond your titles and roles.

- What role did your lost loved one play in your life?

- How do you see yourself? Pretend you are describing yourself to someone who has never met you. For example, are you outgoing, generous, thoughtful, optimistic? Are you a quiet observer or a gregarious talker? Do you like to travel or would you rather read quietly at home? Or do you like to do both? Do you like being around big groups of people or would you rather have dinner with one special friend? Do you like to create things or do you prefer to enjoy things created by others?

- What are some favorite interests and hobbies that bring you joy?

- What new activity or hobby have you explored recently?

- What new activity or hobby would you like to try?

- As an outsider who has watched a family or friend lose a close loved one, what changes have you noticed the most?

- Have you struggled to know how to maintain your relationship with that person?

- Do you feel like you have made enough effort to understand where that person is on his or her journey with a new identity?

CHAPTER 7

Grieving Always

In its simplest terms, grief is the human emotional response to loss, but it's far more complex than that. The way individuals experience and express grief varies greatly, and dictionary definitions of the word "grief" do not define what it feels like to experience a devastating loss. There are no words that can fully express the loss of a loved one. If you search the English language for words that describe grief, you will never find one that gets close to putting a finger on the pulse of what it *feels* like.

CAREY

Grief is an intensely personal emotion. Everyone's grieving process is unique and can vary greatly depending on the individual and the type of loss. The grief I have over losing my husband has been a completely different experience than what I feel from losing my son, who had his whole life ahead of him.

Grief can present in many ways, but we often try to pack it neatly into a one-size-fits-all box. Because of this, we can sympathize with someone's grief, but we can't fully empathize, even if we have suffered terrible losses ourselves. No one will experience and express grief the same way you do, even close friends and family members. You are the only one who has had the unique relationships and personal experiences with the loved ones who are gone. You are the only one who will totally understand your loss.

For me, there are layers of grief. Some layers are obvious and expected. They are the little pings, the small daily reminders of Ross and Cole. I live in Arizona near where Cole lived, and I pass by many places Cole loved and frequented and places we enjoyed together. Seeing those places grabs me with a mini attack of grief. I have learned to manage these episodes when I pass those expected places—until something unexpected triggers an eruption of a far deeper layer of grief. One such event occurred during the holiday season when I walked past the men's clothing section in a department store and remembered how I had always bought new shirts for Ross for Christmas. The memory triggered an emotional meltdown I had not anticipated.

This deep layer of grief erupts out of nowhere, a sneak attack that sucker-punches me in the gut. It knocks the wind out of me, leaving me gasping as if I will never catch my breath again. I can't anticipate or brace myself for all the unexpected triggers that can occur, and sometimes there is no trigger at all. I'm strapped on a roller coaster without a defined beginning or ending point. It is what it is.

On the deepest level, grief has become a part of me, like blood flowing through my body. People commonly describe it as a weight pressing down on you. I feel like it's an extra limb I have grown—always there and never going away. Just after the deaths of Ross and Cole, I was aware of it all the time. I slowly stopped thinking about it constantly, but grief is always present on an unconscious level and will remain a part of me.

My days are bookended with grief. Every day I wake up with the tragedy and go to bed with the tragedy. In the morning, I take a few quiet moments to work through the sadness, get my head on straight, and focus on the bigger perspective, such things as gratitude, purpose, and joy, so I can move on with my day. I think about Cole and Ross again when I go to bed. It's a cycle. Some days I function well. Other days, grief creeps up on me. I feel low and don't know why, and I have a hard time getting my head into the game of what my life is now.

Laurel and I have had to give ourselves a lot of space and time to grieve. Some people say the first year after a loss is the hardest, and in some ways, it was because we were still in shock and adjusting to our new lives. One of the biggest challenges in the first year was dealing with the big events: the first birthdays and holidays without Ross and Cole. A friend of my mine who lost her husband in a car accident more than twenty years ago told me that the first year was tough for her, but the seventh year without him was the hardest. Her husband had died just after their daughter had been born. Perhaps the seventh year after his death was the hardest because she had experienced so many milestones in their daughter's childhood without him. Maybe that year was the most difficult because their daughter had reached the age in which she realized she did not have a father.

It's common for people to mourn for the things a lost loved one will miss in life and for the events that won't happen. I am saddened over these things too, but I also see them a bit differently. I don't believe Ross and Cole are missing us. In my mind, they are still here with us and for us. We see their presence in so many ways and signs; we just can't see or hear them in a tangible way. I know they are in a place that is better than this Earth. They are not missing anything at all; we are just missing them. That is my loss and my grief.

LAUREL

When my dad died, I was hurled from the secure college world at Oklahoma State into a realm of chaos in Colorado. I struggled to get through the funeral and wasn't paying attention to what was going on within me. My body, mind, and emotions were working overtime—with no relief in sight. I am not a person who expresses or verbalizes sadness or feeling bad, and by not talking about my feelings, I was trapping all the negative emotions inside. The internal buildup of unexpressed grief grew as heavy as someone sitting on my chest. It disrupted my mind, body, and spirit to such an extent I also experienced sleep disturbance and digestive issues, such as frequent stomach pain. At the same time, I was eating poorly and not taking care of myself. I was young, blindsided by unexpected tragedy, and in such an intense state of shock, I didn't know how to deal with it.

Everything crashed down around me when my mom started talking about selling my childhood home and moving from Colorado to Arizona to be near Cole. Too many things were happening too fast, and I felt like I was not a part of them. I assumed that I would be returning to a consistent life at college, but everything else in my life was changing, and I couldn't do anything about it. One night in the kitchen, I lost it. I was screaming and crying because I didn't want Mom to move or to lose my childhood home. I couldn't deal with any more change. My mom and Cole were both shocked, but they remained calm because I was a mess. I was sitting on the counter having a meltdown, and they both stood across the room from me letting me get it all out. My life was spinning out of control. Amid the upheaval, I questioned if I should even return to college. I had never experienced so much disruption to my world at one time, and it all came out in that episode of rage.

The next morning, I felt a great sense of relief emotionally and physically. I realized that I had needed to allow myself to grieve and talk about my emotions and not trap them to simmer inside me. Expressing my emotions had helped me come to terms with what was happening. My head cleared, and I decided to return to college.

College provided a normal consistency in my life but could not change the fact that my family would never be the same. When I saw other families together with both parents and all their siblings, it was (and still is) hard not to compare my new life with theirs. Everywhere I went, it seemed other families were happily all together. Their togetherness seemed to jump out from the crowd because that's what I was missing. I found some consolation from talking to others who had lost family members and who also found themselves comparing other families' situations to theirs.

What saddens me the most about the loss of my dad is knowing he will miss out on my future. His death ripped a huge hole through all the important life events I had anticipated. One of the first things I thought about was that my dad would not be at my wedding. As a young girl and woman, I envisioned marriage as a pivotal moment in my life. I could not have imagined walking down the aisle without my dad at my side to give me away. It devastated me to think he would not be able to share the experience with family, friends, and me. After that initial thought, more of my future flashed before my eyes—my college graduation, the birth of my children—all the important moments of my life when my dad would be absent.

It is ironic that I now work in the wedding and event industry. I often witness young brides walking down the aisle with their fathers, and those are the moments I miss my dad the most. When I got married, I chose to walk down the aisle by myself at my wedding because no one else could fill that spot for me.

The hole I felt in my life after my dad died was no less painful at smaller events, such as Dad's Day at college. Dad's Day was a big occasion when fathers shared special campus events with their college kids. For two years, I had to find a way to get through it emotionally without my father. As that first Dad's Day approached, I realized how tough it was going to be for me to be in the middle of those festivities without him, so I chose to leave campus. Instead, I visited my mom and spent the day with her. When the following Dad's Day approached, I decided to stay. At that point, I needed to face it. I had come to understand that those types of events were going to continue to happen, like the graduation and the wedding in which my dad would not take part. I knew I could no longer avoid them and was ready to take on the emotional roller coaster.

While my dad misses out on my milestones, Cole is missing out on his own milestones. I am older now than Cole was when he died, so I grieve the most for all the things he will miss in his life that I will get to do and that my dad did in his life. I also mourn that Cole and I will no longer be able to share our lives as siblings.

Growing up with my big brother was one of the greatest memories of my childhood. He was my best friend and we were inseparable. Just two years apart in age, we were different, yet similar in many ways.

Cole was the creative, patient, and consistent one, and I was the one who couldn't sit still for more than five minutes. He found his favorite sport of tennis at a young age and excelled while I bounced around trying all the sports I could. I always envied that he found his niche in sports, but he supported me in anything I did, coming to many of my events, and I would beam when I felt his approval.

We balanced each other in the best ways and would do anything for each other. I always wanted to keep up with what he was doing, which led me to be a bit of a tomboy. We would make up games in the backyard or flick marbles at army men. We once slept in a box for a week because, why not?

Cole was also my protector. He once ripped a chunk of hair off the head of a guy who insisted on giving me unwanted attention. Cole was not a fighter by nature at all, but when it came to his little sister, the big brother instinct kicked in quickly.

Cole was a big-picture thinker who had a love for capturing the world from behind a lens. He would come up with ideas for videos all the time and would sometimes cast me in them. Many of them were funny, and we would laugh to the point of breathlessness. I'm so thankful today that God gave him that gift; now I can look back both at the videos and the memories we made.

Because of Cole, I view the world differently. He taught me to look beyond what's in front of me and to see and appreciate how beautiful this world can be. He pushed me to be more adventurous and to go beyond my comfort zone. I would give anything to go on one more adventure with him, but for now I will treasure the ones we did go on. At the same time, having great memories makes it harder to come to grips with what I have lost, such as growing together as young adult siblings and maturing into middle age and beyond. We would have likely shared the joy of having our own children and expanding the extended family. I know what it is like now to get married and experience the small moments and big milestones of life, and it saddens me to think he won't experience any more of them.

At the same time, I cherish the special moments we did share—even though they can trigger intense emotions. One special memory is the camping trips Cole and I shared with our dad, when he would teach us outdoor skills and self-reliance. At the end of each full day in the sun, we sat under a sky full of stars and enjoyed the stillness together.

I remember when Cole and I hit adolescence and were too "cool" to hang with our parents—or we pretended to be. In reality, it never bothered me to run around town and hang out with my dad, but I felt I had to keep up the typical teenage persona. To combat this, my dad invented ways to convince Cole and me to run errands with him. One of his methods was to offer a treat of our choice at the car wash. I often chose beef jerky, and my dad would snag a bag of peanut M&Ms for himself. He claimed he didn't have a sweet tooth, so to him, that yellow bag of peanuts covered with chocolate and a sugary shell didn't fall into the "sweets" category. Car washes, peanut M&Ms, and beef jerky became our thing. Together they helped us share consistent, little moments that didn't seem that significant at the time but became lasting memories. Over time, bags of peanut M&Ms would end up in Dad's Christmas stocking, in his birthday boxes, and on road trips to the mountains. They were a symbol of simple pleasures and memories.

After my dad died, my brother started taking a bag of peanut M&Ms to work every day. I believed it was his way of carrying a small piece of my dad with him, but I never asked him about it. We both understood the unspoken meaning behind the candy.

Now that my dad and brother are both gone, I can hardly stand seeing the special treat. The first time I saw peanut M&Ms at a Target after they had passed away, it triggered intense feelings that are almost impossible to describe but are somewhat similar to those of post-traumatic stress disorder (PTSD). Every negative emotion erupted at one time, and I couldn't run from any of them. I wanted to rip open every stupid bag of candy and scream at whoever had put them there. *How dare you remind me of my grief? How could you inflict such pain?* I would never go to the car wash with my dad and brother again and share peanut M&Ms and beef jerky, and I was furious there was absolutely nothing I could do about that. I felt utterly helpless and an overwhelming, frustrating, loss of control.

I used to joke that God didn't give me tear ducts, because I rarely cried. But that day, just the sight of the iconic yellow bag brought me to tears in the middle of a Target aisle. If you've ever gone from zero to a hundred on the emotion scale in a split second, you feel me on this one.

When these episodes first happened, I thought I was going crazy. I had believed people who suffered great losses curled up in bed for a few days, feeling nothing but sadness. How little I knew! When my turn came to walk through my tragic loss, a large dose of reality smacked me in the face. I wasn't sad; I was angry, and I had more anger than I could control at times. I believe that was partially due to the nature of my dad's and brother's deaths, but it also was because anger was my dominant negative emotion.

When my brother called to tell me that my dad had taken his own life, I blacked out. The next thing I remembered was sitting on the floor next to a broken window surrounded by shattered glass. I had punched through the window with my bare hand. It was as if some supernatural fury had taken control of me. I did not cry until after Cole and I had left the police station with Dad's belongings. Three years later, when Cole died by suicide, I was so furious my whole body shook violently. Cole had *promised* me he would not do that to me, and I was angry I had to go through those emotions again. I couldn't do anything but be angry and had a hard time letting go of that. So often I hear the words, "It gets better with time," but time isn't going to bring them back, put my family back together, or erase the memories. What time can do is allow me to learn to cope more effectively. Grieving does not necessarily get easier; it just becomes the new normal.

As time has passed, I have become more aware of things that trigger emotions for me. Despite them, I embrace the cherished memories. It's a difficult balancing act, and I don't think the pain will ever fully go away. As of the writing of this book, it's been almost five years since my dad left this Earth and almost two years since my brother joined him. It hasn't gotten easier; it's just become different, and I have learned how to manage my anger and grief better. I give myself more time now when I do feel down. I allow myself to experience feelings when they occur so they don't build up. I also talk more openly about the way I am feeling and do not shy away from deep, hard-stuff conversations with close friends and family.

I have also learned that it is in my nature to want to justify everything—especially emotions. I still question myself when I feel bad, as if there is a requirement to have a valid, logical reason to feel that way. Then I remind myself that there will be days when I will feel bad without any obvious reason. It happens, and that's fine. I have learned to recognize and accept the feelings and not have to justify them to myself or anyone else.

The results have been eye opening. I am more in tune with myself than I have ever been. I have come to realize the meltdown I had in Target over the peanut M&Ms wasn't so out of line or unexpected after all. A friend of mine who lost her mom is triggered into despair by seeing her mom's favorite style of ankle socks. For another friend, it's hearing a beloved song her grandfather used to sing. These little details of life mean different things to each of us but bring up similar and relatable feelings.

People have asked me how I can be so strong, and that has planted a seed of self-expectation that I always have to be strong. I have had to learn to accept that I do not always have to be strong. In fact, it's impossible and unrealistic. There are days that are harder, but that's normal and part of the process. Even years later, I still have those days.

Looking back now, I am thankful for the first twenty years of my life before suicide touched our family. My dad was involved in every aspect of my life and had a huge influence on shaping my identity. Whether it was an elementary school talent show, Halloween, or even college date parties, I could always count on my dad to have the best ideas to enliven the event. I remember my dad sending me all the Colorado gear he could find when I was a freshman at Oklahoma State for an event that involved dressing up as your home state. He made sure I represented his favorite state proudly. My dad and I also shared a strong desire to lead children to Christ and taught a Sunday school class together. It was one of his passions, and he loved those kids.

People often get angry with God after losing someone they love. They can't understand why God would let such horrible things happen. I understand this feeling, but I have come to see that if this world were perfect, there would be no reason to have faith. When my dad died, I did not want to go to church because of the memories of us going as a family, but I never lost my faith or got angry with God. After Cole died, I felt that going to church would be the only way I could get through it. I did question a lot of things, but overall my faith grew through this experience.

I started teaching Sunday school again because that was something I had done with my dad, and it was a way to begin to heal—to confront something that was painful for me. The first day of class was hard to face, but I quickly connected with a three-year-old girl who was quietly sitting by herself, isolated from the other kids. She sat on my lap and one of the other leaders later told me that the girl was a foster child who didn't connect with people. For me, that was God's way of telling me I was doing something that was glorifying Him, honoring my father's legacy, and healing myself in the process.

No one can tell you the right way to grieve and heal. No matter how many self-help books you read, you still have to find your own path after loss. I don't have the answer for you in this book either, but I can tell you it's vital to care for your mind, body, and spirit without justifying yourself. It is OK—and necessary—to grieve in your own way.

REFLECTIONS AND QUESTIONS TO CONSIDER

Grief is a universal emotion, yet at the same time every individual experiences and expresses it in his or her own way. Below are some questions to ask yourself or discuss within your family and circles of friends to learn more about how you and those close to you grieve. Think about the times you have experienced the loss of a loved one and ask yourself:

- What does grief feel like to you?

- How do you express your emotions when you are grieving?

- Did grieving ever make you feel physically ill? How so?

- What types of activities or actions have helped you express and come to terms with your grief?

- How can you support others who are struggling with loss and grief?

CHAPTER 8

Grace and Mercy

Grace and mercy are critical aspects of the healing process. They are multifaceted gifts that include dropping judgment and extending kindness and forgiveness to those who might be cruel, critical, offensive, or unhelpful. To be truly therapeutic, these gifts must be given with an open heart without the expectation the receiver will pay you back. After tragedy, you may need to give grace and mercy to strangers, people you know, and yourself.

CAREY

Healing takes more time than I had thought and has

required a large dose of grace and mercy. After Cole and Ross died, I continued to work but only as much as was absolutely necessary to fulfill prior obligations. I shelved plans for many projects and left them incomplete for a year. Eventually, I wanted to be productive and active in the real world, so I pushed myself until I hit a wall and had to retreat. I am the queen of this behavior, which makes my life a roller coaster. Since then, when I experience this kind of exhaustion, I have to give myself a break and remember that I'm not running on all cylinders yet. I must accept that I won't be up for attending every social event or hitting as many goals as I once had been. I have to take time to rest, give myself self-love, and be OK with not pushing through.

This is frustrating because I work as a speaker and business coach who inspires people to find their purpose and reach their goals. During the time I took off, it was hard at times for me to not be out there doing what I do. However, I have found that if I don't give myself the grace and mercy to take a break, I won't be capable of helping anyone else.

I have also had to work on giving grace and mercy to Cole and Ross. One day about a week after Ross's death, Laurel and I were moving a large load of stuff to a storage unit. It was heavy, and we struggled to control the cart. It got away from us and rolled across the parking lot. We scrambled to catch it, but I tripped over a parking pillar, fell, ripped my pants, and skinned both my knees. The cart smashed into a parked car, making a huge dent.

I was furious! I was seething! In that moment, I wanted to throw my anger at something, anything. I was having a human moment—and I have them more often than I would like. At the time, I was angry at Ross, although I know that he did not intend to hurt us. In that moment, though, with my scraped, stinging knees, I was frustrated and needed to shake my first at someone. My real frustration was in realizing how much pain Ross had been in and that he couldn't share it, even with those he loved the most. After Cole died, I had the same frustration. I eventually had to understand they were unable to share their feelings with us and let us help them.

Laurel and I must often remind ourselves that their deaths had nothing to do with us. They didn't do it *to* us. People who take their own lives are hurting so much they are often afraid they are causing pain to their loved ones. They can think of nothing else and want to try to save their loved ones from their suffering. A key part of healing for me has been to understand this in my heart.

It has also been challenging, but necessary, to offer grace and mercy to others. After Ross and Cole died, we were bombarded with advice about what we should do.

I listened to all the advice with a smile on my face, but in the end, I often did the opposite of what friends and family recommended, such as not making any major life changes right away. I had to do what I thought was best for us at the time, which included selling the family home in Colorado and moving to Arizona to be close to Cole after Ross died. At first, some of the advice we received felt like it was coming from a place of negativity, which was confusing and made us angry. We eventually saw that most people's recommendations were not meant to hurt us; they just didn't know what else to do for us, or they honestly felt they were offering the best help they could. Most of the people who offered guidance did it out of love. They were simply trying to support us to make the best decisions we could.

After Cole died, I spent big chunks of time living in Oklahoma with Laurel and Ethan, who had moved in together. Not everyone understood the living decisions we made then. Unable to empathize with what we were going through, some people questioned us and recommended what *they* thought was best for us. They didn't see how we were hanging by a thread and needed to be together *as much as possible*, which is true to this day. Laurel and I have always been close. The tragedy did not throw us together, clinging to each other because we "had" to. Our immediate family has always enjoyed being together in many ways, such as traveling and having great conversations, and Ethan fit right in.

Laurel and I have also synced our phones so we can see where the other one is at any time. To this day, we worry if one of us texts and the other one doesn't respond quickly. We get more anxious the longer it takes because we need to feel connected and together at all times in a way not everyone can comprehend.

Many times, we have had to forgive people who have said inappropriate things, such as starting a conversation about suicide at a dinner party. They don't understand that it's the wrong topic at the wrong time. We realized people don't know what they don't know, so we began to empathize and accept those who do not have the capacity to be our super-safe people.

I have learned the most about grace and mercy from the people who have given it to us. Some people have a natural gift of compassion and empathy. I call them my prayer warriors. When they tell me they are praying for me, I know they are on their knees and won't stop. They and others like them go above and beyond and understand my weaknesses. When I get irritable, they don't care. They love me anyway and continue to support Laurel and me no matter what we have chosen to do with our lives. They also gave us space when they didn't feel we were letting them in the way they had expected. Some people became resentful or hurt over these things, but others have continued to love me no matter what I have needed, how much pain I was in, or how ugly I got at some points. They are my biggest inspirations for following their example and giving grace and mercy to others.

LAUREL

A big part of the healing process for me was learning how to forgive people who could not possibly understand what I was going through. After my dad died, certain friends I thought would jump through hoops for me didn't. I had assumed they would because I would have done that for them. On the other hand, some people tried to support us with the best of intentions but ended up doing things that were not helpful. I became resentful of both those who were trying to help in misguided ways and those who were not doing as much as I expected. It wasn't right to feel that way, but I did, and it was not fair to any of them.

I had to learn much about grace and mercy. I now understand that a friend or family member may not know what to do in a time of tragedy but still want to be there for me. It was a difficult process, but I came to see that even when people weren't doing what I expected or wanted, they were showing love and trying in their own way. I had to reevaluate myself and my expectations and embrace what others could give me.

I also have reconsidered some of my friendships. I had been thrown into a different place in my life and forced to grow up fast and be a different person. This had a big impact on my relationships. Some friends could not comprehend why I had changed and was doing things differently, but I came to understand that was because they had not experienced what I was going through. However, if a friendship didn't fit as it once had or didn't bring me a sense of peace, I let it go. The agony of ending a friendship was intensified because I had already gone through huge losses with the deaths of my dad and brother and I didn't want to lose anyone else. Feeling that additional loss made me angry at first, and I agonized over it. However, I needed to let some friendships go and understand and forgive those people for no longer fitting into my life and my healing process.

When I removed people from my life, I felt guilty at first. I believed there was something wrong with me and that maybe I was becoming a bitter person who would not be capable of having friends anymore. I had to give myself grace and mercy when I couldn't be the person I used to be and decided to let some friendships go. I found I had to connect with people in a different way.

After Cole died, I made some quick decisions about my life, including deciding to move in with my fiancé Ethan before marriage. I never would have done that before losing my dad and brother, but I don't regret it because at that point in my life, I needed to be close to Ethan. We also invited my mom to move in with us, and she did. Both Ethan and I loved living together and having my mom there with us. Unfortunately, we got backlash about it on religious and moral grounds, and some people told us they thought it was simply a bad idea. Others thought it was odd that my mom was living with us.

When we made those decisions, we were thinking about what we needed to do for ourselves and not how people would judge us. I had to let the judgments go because the three of us needed to be together. I understood where those opinions were coming from, and under normal circumstances I would have agreed, but nothing was normal anymore. The things some people chose to focus on after we experienced such a tragedy was tough for me to accept, but I could not expect others to understand how we felt at that time.

It was difficult to know what kind of feedback to expect from people. After the negative comments we received about moving in together, I had expected to get more backlash when Ethan and I got engaged so soon after Cole's death. Surprisingly, that did not happen. I never knew what people would talk about or react to the most, so I had to try to take everything as it came, realizing that no one would ever truly understand how I was feeling. The experience taught me a lot about having empathy for others. I came to realize that even if someone had lost a family member to suicide, I would not understand *exactly* how that person felt and what he or she needed to do to heal.

I have learned to be more empathetic in many situations. For example, I was very involved with competitive cheerleading when I was growing up. It is a tougher sport than many realize, and the cheerleading community has a stoic mentality. A cheerleader who falls or gets injured is assumed to be fine, even if he or she has a bleeding head injury. Cheerleaders are expected to jump back up after getting hurt—with a smile on their face. I had accepted that culture and couldn't understand it when someone didn't get back up after they fell.

This mentality bled over into my life after I received the devastating blows that my dad and brother committed suicide. I now understand what someone is really telling me when he or she says they are not OK and they can't get right back up. I can empathize with those who tell me they are still struggling with a physical, mental, or emotional injury, even if it is months or years after it occurred.

I also learned that after a tragedy, friends and family who are initially supportive eventually go back to their everyday lives. I could not be mad when some friends and family stopped reaching out to me weeks and months later; I had done that in the past for others who had suffered a tragedy because I had not understood how important my continued support was to them. Now I know how much I can help someone by continuing to stay in touch after tragedy. My phone call might come at the moment someone is feeling alone and struggling with a loss that other people think they have gotten over a long time before.

I also have had to give myself grace in order to get the rest I needed to heal. I have always been a busy person and like to be involved in many activities and projects. Since the deaths of my dad and brother, I can't always maintain that level of energy and enthusiasm. I have to remind myself that, no matter how much time has passed, there will be days when I need extra time to take care of myself; this is difficult with a personality that doesn't rest.

To help myself rest enough to heal, I decided to work part time instead of full time for a while after Cole died. I was a new adult trying to figure out so many things, and I never knew where my energy level would be. I realized I could handle only a simple part-time job in a gift shop in an event venue. I was still dabbling in wedding planning, but it was a slow-paced year for me. Slowing down and taking a step back in building my career was difficult because I had been a driven person who always had goals and solid plans to reach them. I had to be OK with people who didn't understand, especially because my peers were all forging ahead, going full steam in starting their careers. I felt as if I had gotten a year or more behind in my life, but taking that time was necessary so I could heal myself. When the time was right, I found the perfect full-time job. By giving myself and others grace and mercy, everything came together exactly when it was supposed to.

REFLECTIONS AND QUESTIONS TO CONSIDER

Giving grace and mercy to yourself and others after tragedy and loss is an important step in the healing process. Below are some questions to ask yourself or discuss within your family and circles of friends to explore this concept and how it can help you and others during bereavement.

Think about something someone has done or said to you that made you angry. Did they intend to be hurtful? Or did they just not understand you or your situation at that moment?

- Think about a time when you have inadvertently hurt someone's feelings or acted in a hurtful way.

How did you feel in that moment? Did you react out of anger, frustration, or misunderstanding? How could you have been a better friend or support person in that situation?

- Do you find it hard to forgive yourself for certain things? If so, what kind of things?

- Describe a time when someone who needed your support offered you grace and mercy when you were unkind or unhelpful. How did that feel?

CHAPTER 9

On Suicide

Suicide is an ugly word to us, and we wish there was a better term for taking one's own life. Suicide is also a highly personal and controversial topic that hits a lot of sensitive points with people. We believe many factors contribute to the suicide epidemic. They include psychological, cultural, and spiritual factors, but we don't have it all figured out. We are still suffering from the pain of two suicides in our family, and we hope sharing our thoughts on suicide may offer some peace and comfort to those who have suffered such a tragic loss in their lives.

CAREY

People often ask me how I am still standing and getting through every day since the deaths of my husband and son. Some also ask if I saw the suicides coming. I find it interesting that anyone would ask that, and I answer it with another question: "Would you, even in a million years, think or let your brain comprehend that someone you love would go that far?" Even as anxious and depressed as Ross and Cole had become, we never thought they would go to that extreme and take their own lives. I believe the people who ask me that question either are struggling with depression themselves or are afraid for someone in their lives. What they might really be asking me is, "What are the signs?"

I can't provide a pat answer to that question. Some people show visible signs of serious depression, anxiety, or emotional trouble. They might talk about suicide, threaten it, or even attempt it. However, that was not the case with Ross and Cole. They covered up their deepest, most severe emotions and never hinted they had thoughts of suicide.

One month after Ross died, comedian Robin Williams committed suicide. No one saw that coming either. To the outside world, he was talented, funny, highly revered, and hugely successful. He seemed to have everything going for him. It was a shock to the world that someone who brought laughter and happiness to so many was suffering from so much despair he took his own life.

Like Robin Williams, Ross, and Cole, people who die by suicide can go to great lengths to create a facade that all is well. They might do it out of pride because they fear what the world will think of them. They might also be trying to protect their loved ones. Many people think suicide is a selfish act, and nothing could be further from the truth. At the end of their lives, Ross and Cole had been carrying the burden of immense pain for months, maybe even years. They started believing it would not get any better and saw how it was negatively affecting the people they loved. I believe Ross wanted to protect us before and after his death. He hid the depth of his distress and meticulously planned his death, thinking through the details to ensure we were well cared for after he was gone. He left a large sum of cash and the keys to our filing cabinets in a box on his desk. He also waited for Cole to get home from his Asia trip, so I would not be alone when he died.

Looking back, I remember having unsettling feelings the last few weeks before Ross died. Sometimes I felt like he was not present, even when we were in the same room. It was eerie, and I worried that the stress he was going through with his job would give him a heart attack. One day I went into his basement office and asked him, "I am not going to come down and find you dead in this chair, am I?" He gave me the strangest look. In hindsight, I see things I could not possibly have seen or understood in the moment. I have friends who have lost husbands and children to suicide, and they tell the same story: They knew their loved ones were struggling, but they didn't know the depth of that struggle.

No one wants to see suicide coming because it's too frightening to think they can't control it. They don't want to believe they have friends or loved ones who might walk out the door and, in an instant, decide that this is their last day.

Although Ross and Cole both took their own lives in the same way, by gunshots, the scenarios were different. Ross's suicide was well thought out; I don't know for how long he had been planning it, and like many people who die by suicide, he did not leave a note. On the other hand, I believe Cole panicked that day of his death. He had just left me to go to work. He had told me he planned to tell his boss that he was resigning so he could take a break to manage his stress, but he snapped and shot himself. I couldn't have seen that coming.

I have done a lot of reading about suicide and find much of what I read is very dark and doesn't tell the whole story. Many people want to slap one label on a "cause" of suicide—mental illness. It's easy to point to a disease because we believe we can, in theory, treat a disease. Other people think it's all about hugs. When one of Laurel's classmates died of suicide, social media was blanketed with posts about how we need to hug our kids more, pay more attention, and listen to them more. People want to think that's all it takes, but it's not that simple.

What do they think I was doing? I was paying attention. I was involved. Our family spent time with each other, laughed a lot, and had fun. We did not have big breaks in communication. We were super close and were there for each other at all times. I spent the last two weeks of Cole's life with him, sorting out his anxiety and helping him discover a new vision for his future. He made a new plan that allowed him to be his true self and make his life what his heart desired. Before Ross's death, I spent months talking to Ross about developing a new path for his career because he had been so unhappy with the direction of his job. We talked about it for what seemed like thousands of hours over many months.

Despite this kind of support and love, some people will not reveal just how dark their thoughts have become. They put on a fresh face and keep moving forward to protect the people closest to them and make it seem like they are doing OK. If the fix was as easy as getting more hugs, having more quality time with family, receiving counseling, or taking antidepressants, there wouldn't be so many suicides.

There are many root causes of suicide that no one wants to talk about, because if we did, it would mean we have to own those causes as a society and a culture and do something about them. I believe our culture is one of the underlying factors. We are raising humans who do not understand their own personalities and their special gifts. We often force our sweet, innocent babies and young children into structures that, little by little, strip them of their authentic personalities.

We also pass down our expectations and baggage to them. That becomes a heavy burden to bear because they come to believe the world will not accept them for who they are, so they put on personalities and create identities they think will please everybody else and help them to succeed. In my heart, I believe Ross's calling was to be a teacher, but his identity had become attached to his sales career. When he was faced with losing the job that had brought him money and success for thirty years, he was lost. His self-esteem took a nosedive, and he had no idea what he would do.

Our culture is focused on success and results above all else, at any cost. The more a family or a community values success and achievement, the harder it is for an individual who thinks that he or she is not living up to expectations to feel connected. The sense of failure to achieve an (unrealistic) level of success creates anxiety and shame and makes it difficult to feel accepted and let people in. I think Ross and Cole had other sides of their personalities they wanted to explore and didn't because they felt they needed to be a certain type of person to achieve success. At Ross's memorial, Cole spoke on behalf of the family. He said he knew that his dad was outside himself when he took that final step to end his life, because he wanted us to remember him for the man he was, not the man who took his life.

As humans we can't get our brains around something we can't easily explain. We will never totally understand why Ross and Cole were called home in this way, but we do know that they touched many people's lives while they were here—more than we realized. After their deaths, many people told us how much Ross and Cole had personally helped them. Cole had a soul that could sense when people needed help, and he had a gift. He was instinctively supportive and could talk people through their problems and issues. Ross also helped a lot of people just by being who he was.

For me, there is a spiritual element to their deaths, and I don't believe mental illness was the main cause of their suicides. For some reason, their time here on Earth was complete, and I have to believe this was God's plan for their life, as hard as that is to understand. God's plan is sovereign, and I have come to trust that. They were meant to be who they were for a short time on Earth and to leave Laurel and me to pick up the ball and continue with their purpose and legacy. It is our mission. As a motivational speaker and vision expert, I am passionate about writing this book and talking to people to help them discover their true purpose in life.

A friend of mine once told me he was intrigued by why people who experienced tragedy often go on a mission. He was not judging us or anyone else with his statement and admitted that he could not possibly understand the feelings and motivations of people who survive tragedies. I told him that after Ross's and Cole's deaths, I had to make a choice. I could either have let their deaths shut me down and remain stagnant in those feelings, or I could decide to use the experience to do good. I had to accept what had happened and make sense out of it.

Laurel and I believe God uses everything for good. There is a reason for it we cannot see now, but we will understand it once we join them on the other side in heaven. God knew all along how Ross and Cole were going to die, but we will never know why He allowed it. It's all a part of His plan, which is baffling to the human mind. It was difficult for me to grasp this idea; I hated it and still wish it had been different. However, it now gives me a lot of peace to know they both were with Jesus the moment they died and are no longer in pain.

LAUREL

When Cole and I talked about our dad's death, he once asked me, "Isn't the thought of killing yourself scary?" I admitted I was terrified to think suicide had become a part of my dad's thought processes—a "logical" solution to his problems. That's when I understood that my dad was not himself in those moments, nor was Cole when he took his own life three years later. I'm frightened to think of what was going through their minds in the last moments of their lives. I have had a hard time coming to terms with that, and I try to remember them as themselves. I know they were hiding their feelings to protect Mom and me; protecting us was an important part of who they were. I wish they hadn't tried so hard to shield us and had let us into their thoughts and shared their emotions more with us. They were probably afraid of what they were feeling, so they defaulted to doing what they naturally did—maintaining a front to spare us.

The police officer who explained my father's death to me told me that when he responded to a suicide call, there were usually obvious signs the victim was in distress. He said people who died from suicide often looked unkempt and dirty, like they had been struggling with their lives for a while. He found the opposite scenario with my dad, who had been freshly showered and immaculately dressed. In Cole's case, he had just gotten a haircut two days before his death. In both cases, they had cared well for themselves until the end.

It seems there are two kinds of people who die by suicide: those whose lives have fallen apart and who have let everything go, and those who are desperately trying to keep their lives together and can't—but put up a front of being fine. For my dad and brother, it seemed they put up the strongest front in their darkest moments so no one would see the depth of their distress. It was as if they were trying to hold things together by staying true to what people had come to expect of them.

We have created a society in which we have to filter many pieces of our lives and personalities in order to make ourselves into something we're not. I believe that leads people to create public personas and lose their true selves in the process. I have fallen victim to it as well—trying to create an image of perfection. The world is not meant to be perfect and neither are we.

People often question why horrible things happen, such as the deaths of my dad and brother. I have had many days in which I ruminated on unanswerable questions, such as "Why did this happen to me?" and "Why

do I have to deal with this pain and loss of my family?"
I have felt like I would never understand it. Over time, I
began to see that if nothing bad ever happened to me, I
would have no reason to have faith in something better.
After the deaths of my dad and brother, this idea was
a sobering and heartbreaking concept to grasp. I had a
difficult time understanding God's plan in this tragedy.
Other causes of death can make people question God
and the reasons for their loss, but they may more easily
eventually see and accept them as God's plan. Because
suicide is self-inflicted, survivors have a far more difficult
time seeing God in what happened.

A counselor once asked me if I believed that Jesus
was present with my dad and brother when they killed
themselves. I told her I couldn't imagine He was there
and allowed it. She then asked me to change my perspective and picture Jesus being there to catch them when
they were no longer strong enough to stand by themselves. I found it frustrating to think that way. If Jesus
was there with them, why did he just *catch* them and not
stop them? That question will never be answered until
I get to heaven myself, but I have come to accept that
there was a reason for their deaths. Before they died, I
thought people who died by suicide were ruining God's
plan. Now I understand that God knows every decision
and sin we are going to make before we make them and

forgives us; it is all a part of His plan, and He will be there to catch us when we fall.

I believe suicide is one of the hardest ways to lose a loved one. People who have lost someone in other ways try to understand, but they can't, because the causes of suicide are not as straightforward as many other types of deaths. For example, losing a loved one in a car accident or to a disease is just as tragic, but those left behind can see a clear cause of their loss. Suicide is far more complicated, and survivors of suicide have to deal with many questions that may never be answered.

People often cringe at the thought of discussing suicide openly or hearing the feelings of those who are thinking about taking their own lives. When people ask how my dad and brother died, I almost don't want to say the word "suicide" too loud because of the reaction I might get. If I were to tell them they died of a disease, no one would flinch in the same way, which is unfortunate considering how common suicide is. I wasn't aware of that, nor of how many people are affected by suicide, until it happened in our family. Now it seems that everyone either has lost a loved one to suicide or knows someone who has. It's so prominent in our society, yet it's not talked about. Talking about suicide needs to become a more normalized conversation, which would allow people to feel comfortable talking about their feelings and confiding in others if they are depressed, anxious, or have suicidal thoughts.

REFLECTIONS AND QUESTIONS TO CONSIDER

The causes and underlying factors that might lead to suicide are not well understood, and there are many pre-conceived ideas and myths that surround the topic. Now that you have read much of our family's story, take some time to ponder your ideas and beliefs about suicide. You can also discuss these questions within your family and circles of friends.

- What opinions did you have of suicide, and its victims and survivors, before reading this story?

- How has the Conley family's story shaped or changed your views and perspective on suicide?

CHAPTER 10

Owning Your Story

This society has created a culture in which people are afraid to be open and honest about themselves and to be vulnerable with others. This environment encourages people to shut down and fabricate an identity and a life they want to project to the world. The result is broken adults raising broken children who become broken adults. This kind of dysfunction perpetuates itself, and that's not working for society.

What does it mean to own your story? And how can owning your story help transform grief into hope?

CAREY

It's natural to want one easy button to push or one magic pill to take to solve these problems instead of looking at ourselves. We have to recognize and own our own dysfunction, so we don't pass it down to the next generation. The reason we struggle to be honest about ourselves and who we are is because of shame. We are ashamed of our mistakes and our self-perceived failures, so instead of sharing them and our feelings about them, we isolate our true selves and don't own our stories.

There are some people who are courageous enough to share their stories of dysfunction and imperfection, but because of that heavy weight of shame, it is hard to do for many of us. When we share our stories and feelings about a mistake we have made, a failure, or something horrific we have experienced, it levels the playing field among all humans. It neutralizes shame, allowing us to relate our own lives to the experiences and feelings of others. The world becomes more connected, and people stop judging each other.

This world needs more people to share their stories if we want to create a culture of healthy, wholehearted people who are happy with who they are. The purpose of writing this book has been for Laurel and me to own our story, so our experiences might make a difference in the lives of others. It would have been far easier for us to curl up, shut down, and not talk about our tragedy. We don't want to own our story; we hate it. But sharing our story and feelings about it has helped us transform our grief—to see outside ourselves and our internal darkness and look up to find the light of hope.

LAUREL

When I was in college, my friends and other students frequently asked about each other's parents and families. After my dad died of suicide, I had to make a choice every time that conversation arose. I could choose either to imply that my parents were both still alive or retell the full story of my dad's death yet again. I often chose the former because I thought it would save me the pain of reliving my loss. The first couple of times I decided to reveal my dad was dead, I lied about how it happened. I once said he died of a heart attack, and another time I said he died in a car accident. I shied away from the truth because I did not want his suicide to be a part of how people saw me. I soon learned to be cautious about when to reveal that detail because I wasn't sure how the truth would be received. I had to be careful whom I opened up to, because I was ashamed.

It took time to overcome shame and get comfortable sharing the truth and being vulnerable to people's reactions. Once I was ready to be honest, I had many unexpected, wonderful conversations, and some that didn't go well at all. However, being vulnerable created a priceless opportunity to touch other people who had also struggled silently with imperfection and shame. Making those connections and helping others have been the silver linings of this experience and have made it easier to deal with the negative conversations when necessary.

Sometimes I think that social media has doomed us all. We have filtered our own lives and those of others through this medium, which tends to encourage us to create and post unrealistic, insincere pictures of perfection. We are always winning and succeeding on social media, which feeds into the illusion and expectation that everything in our lives has to be perfect, and that there is something wrong and unfixable with you if you do not achieve the impossible.

Once I allowed myself to be publicly vulnerable and I shared my true story and my true feelings, I found that people wanted more of it. They craved seeing and relating to a human being human. Connecting with others like yourself is like taking a breath of fresh air for the first time in a long time.

So, why are we not doing this more on social media? Why are we not being more real? Why are we afraid of our own stories and shying away from owning them?

I still have days when I become preoccupied with

myself. I want to deny what has happened to our family. I get angry about my life now and yearn for everything to be as it once was. I start to fall into a dark hole and have a pity party, but I give myself a little grace knowing I need to occasionally have those moments. Then I remind myself what's important. Do I move forward, own my story, and do something positive with it, or do I stay in the dark hole? I remind myself that there are many people who have experienced tragedies that are as bad or worse than mine. I realize that I can be the person who brings a breath of fresh air to those who suffer in dark silence from shame and the pain of grief and loss. I can be a vessel for God's purpose, and that's the greatest comfort—and triumph—of all.

REFLECTIONS AND QUESTIONS TO CONSIDER

Owning your story can take practice, but it can also free you from the pain and loneliness of shame and connect you to others who also suffer in silence and help them. Here are some ideas to consider by yourself. You can also discuss these questions within your family and circles of friends.

- How do I like to portray myself to the world?

- Do I feel embarrassed or ashamed of things I like, activities I enjoy, or goals I want to achieve?

- Do I feel a need to fulfill everyone else's expectations?

- Am I comfortable admitting and discussing my failures and faults?

- How can I own my own story?

CHAPTER 11

Finding Heaven on Earth

People often have a vague perception of what heaven is. Many picture heaven or the afterlife as a celestial space located beyond the clouds or in a distant galaxy. However, there are signs everywhere we are already living within heaven. God is in everything we experience with our senses every day. There is no separation or vast distance, but when people force a division between God and heaven and themselves, the results trickle down into daily life. It causes a disconnection among them and within themselves, a detachment from who they are and their purpose in life. Souls are left adrift, forcing individuals to cope with tragedy and loss without an anchor. Finding God and heaven within ourselves and our present world is the key to navigating the loss and grief of this world with the promise of hope in this life and the next.

You don't need to have a Christian perspective on heaven like we do for this idea to help you. It works for those who have other religious beliefs about the afterlife and for those who have a scientific belief in the infinite universe.

CAREY

Not long after Cole died, a friend of ours from high school contacted me and told me that Ross had visited her in a dream. He told her to tell me he had never left me and was always with me. She said the dream was vivid, and she was emphatic that Ross had insisted she pass along the message.

This story is one of many told by friends and family that have helped me understand we are sitting in the middle of heaven, right now, in this moment. Heaven and our lost loved ones are *here* with us; Earth is inside of heaven. We are surrounded by heaven, and everything we see gives us a glimpse of it. At the same time, heaven's vastness is on the other side of a door in a space we cannot see.

The suicides of Ross and Cole were so violent and tragic the negativity could have destroyed Laurel and me.

We could have easily fallen into a destructive pattern of ruminating on our own despair. We had to find a different perspective or we would not have survived. Our answer lay in finding a focal point in our lives that was bigger than ourselves. We chose two Bible verses:

For our light and momentary troubles are achieving for us an eternal glory that far outweighs them all.
—2 Corinthians 4:17

So we fix our eyes not on what is seen, but on what is unseen, since what is seen is temporary, but what is unseen is eternal.
—2 Corinthians 4:18

These Bible verses have provided us with great meaning and perspective, and they help us focus on the things that are unseen and eternal instead of what is seen and temporary. Our anchor has become a heavenly perspective. I don't know how people survive life's adversities and tragedies and find peace or joy without it. The only thing that gets me through is knowing that this day is just a small blip on the radar of a much larger, eternal life. Knowing this gives me peace.

In our culture, we do not talk much about heaven. Even in churches, heaven is often not discussed as much as it should be, which is sad because it's the only thing that is important. Life is not about our stuff, the people we know, or our successes; heaven is the reason for everything—the ultimate goal.

We should often ask ourselves: "What's tripping me up and getting me down?" The answer is often "stuff"—materialistic, superficial things and pursuits. We easily get tied up with the little stuff that doesn't matter. When we can't pinpoint why we aren't feeling more joyful, we try to fill the void with more stuff, which doesn't fix anything. Then when tragedy and loss come, stuff and success mean nothing. Now when Laurel and I worry about things or events, we remind ourselves that no one we know died today and that this incident is not a big deal. We have been through the worst, and this blip on the radar is nothing. Having a vision of heaven is the only mainstay in weathering all of life's storms.

Cole had an instinctively healthy perspective about heaven. He was naturally unattached to the stuff of this world. Even as a young boy, he intuitively understood that we would all be together forever. After Ross died, he reminded me frequently that Ross was still with us, that we were all already inside heaven, and that there was only a door between Ross and us.

One Christmas after Cole's death, Laurel had a pillow made for me out of one of his favorite tennis shirts.

The woman who made the pillow said she felt someone's hand on her shoulder while she was working on it, and she heard a clear message:

Everything is good, and everything will all make sense when you are on the other side. Nothing is without purpose. I'm sorry for all of the sorrow I caused you. Life is worth living.

She also sensed that Cole was telling her exactly how he wanted the pillow to be made. She felt his presence the entire time. Laurel had no idea that would happen. She simply thought the pillow would be a great gift for me.

Now we are so attuned to the signs that God and heaven are all around us that they don't surprise us anymore. For example, Cole and I loved sunsets and enjoyed watching them together. Not long ago, I was watching a beautiful sunset from my balcony when a restaurant below me began playing the Latin song "Besame Mucho." The title means "kiss me a lot," and it was one of Ross's favorite songs. Another example is when I hear birds sing in the morning; it is as if Ross is here with me and can't stop talking. It makes me smile.

It is easy to get caught up with what's missing in life. When I'm feeling down about losing my husband and son, I have to remind myself that my grief isn't *it*. Grief is just one emotion in one moment of one day. I cannot change what has happened, but I can keep looking up from my everyday troubles and seeing the light that is Ross and Cole, the light of what is still to come for us all. I have a mantra I repeat to myself over and over that helps get me through the days: *Together forever and better than before.* When I find myself focusing on my loss and how much I'm missing them, I use my mantra to think about how we will all be together forever in heaven, and it will be better than it ever was. Not only does this help me cope on a daily basis, it gets me super excited about the future.

It's all about the big perspective, the great universe, and the connection between all mankind. In my vision, heaven is a place that is unimaginably better than it is on Earth because we will be together there, and all of our pain will be gone. It carries me through the day to know exactly where I'm going the moment I die. I know we are together, here and now, and will be forever. I know that after my own death, our togetherness will be infinitely better than it ever was. I am confident of this because the Bible has promised it to me. This promise is a beautiful gift that enlightens the darkest moments I have, and I am so sure of it that half of my heart is already in heaven with Ross and Cole.

When we become aware the world is temporal and look up to something bigger, we see things differently. We stop obsessing about materialistic stuff and petty dramas and experience a life that is infinite. We experience the divine. People naturally fear death because it is an unknown, but I'm not afraid. In this life, I can already see what is on the other side, and I am excited about it.

LAUREL

I grew up in a Christian household in which our family accepted Jesus as our savior. To this day, I have faith I will get into heaven because I believe that Jesus is my savior. I have always believed it is a beautiful place and that my whole family and I would go there and be together after we pass away. After my dad died from suicide, it upset me horribly to think that maybe he would not go join with God because he took his own life. I was afraid he had ruined God's plan for him and would not get into His Kingdom. At first, I was so distraught about it, I couldn't bring myself to ask the question, "Did Dad go to heaven?" I was terrified of what the answer might be.

Then when planning my dad's funeral, a pastor asked us what we were struggling with or if we had any questions. I do not know why, but at that moment, I was able to express my deepest fear and ask the question— the most difficult question I have ever asked. I held my breath, feeling like all the air had been sucked out of the room while I waited for his answer.

"Do you believe that God forgives our sins?" the pastor asked.

"I do."

"Have you ever done something that you feel would bar you from getting into heaven?"

"No."

He smiled and said simply, "Then why would it be any different for your dad's sins?"

That was all I needed to know. It made perfect sense and rang true to what I had been raised to believe—that every sin is equal in God's eyes. That pastor gave me peace and reassurance that my dad was in heaven and would be there waiting for us when the rest of the family and I joined him someday.

Before my dad died, I believed heaven was a faraway place, an esoteric concept that did not have meaning for me. After I lost my dad, I started to notice traces of God's Kingdom in my everyday life. It appeared to me in the ordinary things I had once ignored or taken for granted, such as monarch butterflies. They weren't occasionally flitting here and there; they appeared everywhere and in unusual places, such as resting on my car and flying close to my face. At first I thought it was a coincidence, but they appeared to me so consistently that I realized it had to mean more. I did some research and found that butterflies, as well as birds, are often associated with angels—enlightening and not entirely surprising. I began to see butterflies as angels and a symbol of my dad and heaven. Whenever I see one now, I know that Dad and Cole are angels and are always with me and protecting me. The flutter of butterfly wings is also a sign that heaven is not some far-off place; it exists on Earth and is all around us in the beautiful things of life. It has always been here—much closer than I had thought. I just had not looked for it before.

After Cole died, Ethan proposed to me with a box of live butterflies. He said it was his way of including my dad and brother in our engagement as we started our new life together. We also released live butterflies at our wedding. They hovered over me and the women in the wedding party and settled in our flowers. Our photos of them were shared widely on Instagram, and the word spread about how I viewed butterflies as angels. Soon, many people were posting about how they were noticing butterflies. Not only was I seeing angels on Earth, but other people were too. I love to share my experiences seeing God's Kingdom on Earth with others, because I don't think people always look for it on their own. It is one small way I can help people see how close God is to them.

Another sign of heaven on Earth is when I see the date 11/11 or the time 11:11. November 11, 1991, is my brother Cole's birthday. Often I will have a sudden urge to look at my watch or a clock, then will find that it's 11:11. In addition, some people believe 11/11 is a lucky number and make a wish when they see it. I also dream a lot about my dad and brother. They are always present in my dreams, and I feel like it's their way of visiting me in my sleep and giving me a few more moments with them until we are together again.

As I have found heaven on Earth and focus more on it, I have come to see how small and insignificant earthly matters really are. Before the deaths of my dad and brother, I got so wrapped up in little things that would often throw me for a loop. Achieving success in college and getting my degree seemed like all that mattered. Those things are important, but my perspective has changed. The promise God has made us about heaven has deep meaning for me, and I now look beyond the immediate and the smaller things at the grand scheme. Everything—good or bad—is temporary and will not last forever.

We can easily get fixated on earthly things, which don't matter in the long run. Because of what I have gone through and learned, I have become less materialistic and more confident of my future beyond this life. My mind has been freed from an earthly fixation, and I hope I can help others achieve this too. Before I lost my dad and brother, I had a veil of ignorance cast over my eyes. Now I want to help others recognize that veil and help them remove it. God and His Kingdom are obvious and all around us on Earth, but we often don't see it. Beautiful mountain views, sunsets, and flying butterflies are God's way of giving us tangible images we can understand. No matter how grand and breathtaking these things can be, they are only small pieces of God's reminder of His promise of everlasting life. When I see the beauty of Earth now, I can't wait to see what it will be like in heaven.

REFLECTIONS AND QUESTIONS TO CONSIDER

Finding heaven on Earth means letting go of earthly "stuff" and looking up to see the bigger vision. Trying to do this can make navigating everyday relationships tricky. Friends and relatives might try to draw you into fluffy or gossipy conversations as an easy diversion from your grief. These kinds of conversations can be a big part of communication and bonding in relationships but may offer little lasting consolation and peace. Most people have experienced a serious loss in their lives, even if they don't appear to want to talk about it. Here are some conversation starters to help you and others look up and find heaven on Earth.

- What activities or things that are not material possessions bring you the most joy in everyday life?

- What brings you a sense of peace?

- What do you see as beautiful in the world?

- Do you have a concept of heaven or the afterlife? Explain.

ACKNOWLEDGMENTS

We want to acknowledge our writing partner, Catherine Spader, for listening to our words and our hearts as we went through this process; our friends and family for their love, prayers, and support; and God for being our rock and promise of heaven.